# Family Feasting

### A celebration of simple recipes for family eating

## John Eley
*'The Cooking Canon'*

Marshalls

Marshalls Paperbacks
Marshall Pickering
3 Beggarwood Lane, Basingstoke, Hants, RG23 7LP, UK
a subsidiary of the Zondervan Corporation Inc.

Copyright © 1985 by John Eley
First published in 1985 by Marshall Morgan & Scott Ltd

**British Library Cataloguing in Publication Data**

Eley, John
Family feasting with the cooking canon.
1. Cookery —
I. Title
641.5          TX652.5

ISBN 0–551–01268–4

Phototypeset in Linotron Garamond
by Input Typesetting Ltd, London
Printed in Great Britain by
Hazell Watson & Viney, Aylesbury, Bucks.

# Contents

# Conversion tables

I tend to work in imperial measures all the time, but if you are more used to the metric system, equivalent measurements are given throughout the book. It is never wise to mix imperial and metric measures in the same recipe.

| Oven temperatures | | | Measurements | | Weights | |
|---|---|---|---|---|---|---|
| Mark 1 | 275°F | 140°C | ⅛ inch | 3 mm | ½ oz | 10 g |
| | 2 300 | 150 | ¼ | ½ cm | 1 | 25 |
| | 3 325 | 170 | ½ | 1 | 1½ | 40 |
| | 4 350 | 180 | ¾ | 2 | 2 | 50 |
| | 5 375 | 190 | 1 | 2.5 | 2½ | 60 |
| | 6 400 | 200 | 1¼ | 3 | 3 | 75 |
| | 7 425 | 220 | 1½ | 4 | 4 | 110 |
| | 8 450 | 230 | 1¾ | 4.5 | 4½ | 125 |
| | 9 475 | 240 | 2 | 5 | 5 | 150 |
| | | | 3 | 7.5 | 6 | 175 |
| | | | 4 | 10 | 7 | 200 |
| **Volume** | | | 5 | 13 | 8 | 225 |
| 2 fl oz | | 55 ml | 6 | 15 | 9 | 250 |
| 3 | | 75 | 7 | 18 | 10 | 275 |
| 5 (¼ pt) | | 150 | 8 | 20 | 12 | 350 |
| ½ pt | | 275 | 9 | 23 | 1 lb | 450 |
| ¾ | | 425 | 10 | 25.5 | 1½ | 700 |
| 1 | | 570 | 11 | 28 | 2 | 900 |
| 1¾ | | 1 litre | 12 | 30 | 3 | 1 kg 350 g |

# Prologue

Which came first – the chicken or the egg? Fortunately, such questions need not trouble the family cook. For most of us, there is little problem other than that of budget and taste, but within those limitations there is always the further problem of how best to offer the family a varied and interesting diet to encourage them to eat well and sensibly. Not an easy task, and I do have great sympathy with many mums who go to great efforts to prepare a meal only to see it demolished in minutes by a hungry family who hardly have time to notice the fact that it has been fitted in among a host of other chores with a great deal of love and expertise, (although the skill is often underestimated by the cook herself!) In this book, I hope to give you some fresh ideas for family meals which everyone under your roof can share in and enjoy, and which make the most of the weekly food budget.

Before we dive into the recipes, let's reflect for a minute upon the 'breaking of bread' in the past.

Eating together as an activity of friendship predates Christianity itself and, I'm sure, can be found in ancient history. There has always been something symbolic about sitting down with friends around a table, sharing a common meal. The gesture says, 'You are most welcome and we wish to share what we have with you' Over a meal we enter into new relationships with people as eating together is one of the most intimate things that we do in public. It is much more than a refuelling stop – it is a social occasion when we experience a little of the give and take necessary to oil the wheels of life. The simple kindness of passing the salt or the plate, and them being received with courtesy, are all signs that as friends and family we accept and respect one another and care for each other's needs. These simple graces are so important to nurture in our all-too-often rushed family life. I often wonder how many families can and do sit down together for a common meal at least once a day? I know for many families, because of long hours and shift work, this is not always possible and nowadays, even the traditional Sunday lunch sit-down together is not always possible. However let me tell you a little of my own experience of family eating.

My experience takes me back to my childhood days in Suffolk, and like so many other people's memories of childhood, I recall the happy moments and the absurd with great joy. We lived miles from anywhere in the middle of a lot of fields in Suffolk and my father was a shepherd. It was through attending the secondary school that I met a clergyman and his family who lived in a village in another part of the county. He taught part-time at the school and I became great friends with one of his sons. They were quite a large family, and my life was never to be the same after knowing them!

In the summer holidays I used to stay with my friend Andrew and his family at the beautiful Georgian Vicarage in Hartest, which was what you might call the perfect mediaeval village with a squire who lived in a splendid house, a beautiful village green, little shop and, of course, the church. In fact it was in this village that the artist Geoffrey

Clarke designed and made the Crown of Thorns for Coventry Cathedral. However there was a strong family influence at the vicarage and every morning we would all sit down together – family and friends – for the breakfast of cereal and boiled eggs. I remember the general kerfuffle each morning as we all shared in the tasks of setting the table, each place with its own individual napkin. During breakfast the Vicar read the paper and afterwards we all helped their mother to do the crossword puzzle in the *Telegraph* (admittedly only the quick crossword). It was not a special occasion, but nevertheless it was an important part of the routine and rhythm of family life. We were all voluntary partakers of it, but there was a discipline involved, and as a family and friends it helped us grow together. As a gastronomic experience I must admit that it was one of my first, as there I became addicted to soft boiled eggs with lots of black pepper and buttered soldier-fingers of toast, plus Kenya coffee . . . to all of which I still have an addiction . . . delicious!

The impression this made on me was reinforced at Sunday lunch time. Despite the natural interruption for church services, Sunday lunch was always provided with ample for the family and a few guests (not forgetting Tigger, the cat). A lasting memory I have is that of Grandpa and his insistent call for salt and our exasperation at trying to get it to him before he had time to ask for it . . . it became a family joke and I can still hear him say 'Salt' in his sonorous tone.

No less today at the vicarage do we manage to organise and celebrate at a couple of services and then have guests for Sunday lunch, quite often one of the couples who are preparing themselves for marriage. We usually get together with another family, children included, to build up relationships trust and love. I never look at this as a 'business' occasion when I entertain the 'parish', but see us as fellow human beings, friends together, and hopefully the Holy Spirit will do the rest . . . that is if the cook has done his!!!

Eating should really and unashamedly be part of the celebration of life. That is why I love the French so much, because without overdoing it they have a reverence for all food and take great care in its preparation and presentation, and do not dismiss it as you would an unwanted gift. They are not pious about it, but there is far more ritual over food in France, and it is central to family living. They give *time* to food, and I sincerely hope that they resist the temptation to shorten their traditional two-hour lunch break in the middle of the day, although this does mean that they have to work later in the evening. A good deal of business work is done over meals in France and if anyone has ever had to do business with a Frenchman, you soon come to realise that we could never match their culinary hospitality on the expense accounts of many companies in this country!

We mark the major events in our lives with some form of special food: the traditional Christmas fare and the wedding breakfast for instance, as well as those sometime 'jolly' meetings together of families after a funeral. Some of these have been more relaxed than some wedding breakfasts I have been to! Indeed I remember one very special occasion when an old Dorset countryman died in the home in which he was born and to which he had brought his bride, having done his courting in the lane that ran by the side of the house, and marrying her in the church at the end of the lane. He was getting on in years when he died and when his end was near he sent for the curate and told him that he would not die until two cuckoos appeared in his garden . . . Spring came and so did the cuckoos and this delightful old gentleman went to meet his Maker. He had a plot reserved for himself and his wife in the local churchyard and had often cut the grass over it to make sure the turf would be neat and ready to be cut when he was ready to go.

The day of the funeral was one of those incredible West Country spring days when the weather started off well but then became torrential. Such was the downpour that before the end of the service, which was attended by such a gathering as would give credit to a Thomas Hardy novel, the undertaker had to nip out of the church and pump out the grave with a stirrup pump. However four large and jolly farmers managed to carry our friend to the grave and lower him in, whilst the curate sank quietly into the nearby mire!

He never left a will, but had always let it be known that we were to see him off with a good drink and a ham sandwich. He had saved up for and purchased a crate of good whiskey for this very special day, and as the rain poured down we trudged back to the cottage at the end of the lane, the cuckoos having fled for a better resting place, and were greeted with doorstep – ham sandwiches and good teacups full of whiskey. It was a party the like of which I will never see again, but it was certainly the way he wanted to go!

We thought it safer to drive the curate and his

scooter back to the town on the tractor and trailer, and the rest of the party decided to join us as well, singing hymns heartily all the way.

Christians are familiar with the Last Supper (or was it the first eucharist? A point that I am not going to debate here.) However that meal itself was part of the celebration of the Jewish Passover Festival and therefore this Christian act of eating together in a religious meal has its roots in Judaism, and this should not surprise us.

There are many rules and regulations which make it quite hard for us to understand the dos and don'ts of Jewish eating and I have very great respect for my orthodox friends who follow the rules with such sincerity. Much of what is allowed is described in the book of Leviticus where it becomes clear that the philosophy of Jewish cooking is more than cold legalities of what can or cannot be eaten, but involves the whole economy of the household and kitchen.

Stepping into the Christian tradition, it would seem that we have been set free from many of the restrictions that would tie us down about food . . . It is not what goes *into* a man that defiles him, the New Testament says.

Early Christians in the second century had a very difficult time worrying over questions of 'unclean' food and food preparation but they seem to have been reassured by their leaders that there were more important things to question. Today, I do not think that the Almighty would have us spend our time worrying about such things either, but I do sometimes feel that there is room for great improvement in our commercial food handling. I loathe the way some supermarkets heap together many of our fine vegetables and fruits which simply ruins them, and then throw them away because they are unsaleable. Staff are so often badly trained or not trained at all and can give no information on what they are selling. Simply saying that there are red potatoes or white is not enough. Every cook needs to know more about the items, their varieties, their origin and their best uses. I would imagine it would make the job of selling more interesting and help our general appreciation and understanding of food. But perhaps I am too idealistic.

The early Christians met on the first day of the week for food, and fellowship and out of these meetings came the formalised Holy Communion and thanksgiving of today: the Eucharist, the Thanksgiving. World history and all religions have always been influenced by the common meal. Hospitality has always been one of the trademarks of many holy people, who always had room for one more . . . even if the others had a little less. St. Benedict had some good things to say about entertaining strangers, 'Some by so doing have entertained Angels', and I sincerely hold firm to the fact that hospitality warmly given can help us in our lives and in our relationships not only towards strangers but also within the family.

We need to find a way to put the family back in its proper position at the centre of our society and what better way to start than by caring and sharing at the table? The aim of this little book is to present some recipes that the family can enjoy together, not just eating them, but in joining in the preparation of them too. Some dishes will be good for parties and festivals, others will involve each member of the family in some part of their making. No one is excused! Cooking can and should be fun for everyone. And remember, try to have a little bit extra at the ready just in case someone should turn up. Brighten their day and yours by sharing your *Family Feast*.

Happy cooking,

John Eley
May 1985.

# Family · Feasting
# STARTERS

'In the beginning . . .'

*Genesis Chapter One*

A selection of tasty dishes that arouse the palate and create some anticipation for the next course.

## RECIPES:

Cream of lettuce soup
Artichoke soup
Celery and leek soup
Crevettes au fromage
Miniature quiches
Sardine savouries
Liver paté
Chicken and sausagemeat terrine
Sardine paté
Button mushroom bake
Stuffed button mushrooms
Stilton dip

A recipe book is a bit like the Bible: if you try to work your way through great chunks of it at once then you suffer chronic indigestion! It has to be looked at in small complementary sections, balanced with the household budget and then used to the best effect possible for the good of your family and other living things under your roof!

Not every meal need commence with a starter, especially informal family meals, and on the other hand some starters really do make a good lunch-time snack on their own.

The three soups we begin with really come into their own when home-made and they are blissfully simple. The great secret is to use prime ingredients and a really good home-made chicken stock. Just to start you off, here is a recipe to keep always to hand:

### Home-made chicken stock
Take the bones from the Sunday chicken and any leftover pieces of meat and place them in a thick saucepan. Add a roughly chopped onion, a roughly diced carrot, some sliced celery if there is any lying around, a bouquet garni and some salt and freshly-ground black pepper. Cover with cold water and simmer *gently* for about three hours. Allow to cool and then strain through a sieve or muslin cloth. The stock should set well provided you have not used too much water and you have not over-boiled it.

This stock will freeze well and at certain times of the year I have a freezer full of it.

The *Crevettes au fromage, Miniature quiches* and *Sardine savouries* really can serve well as a lunchtime or supper snack in themselves. Many of my recipes have come to me via many friends but the sardine recipe was the favourite teatime dish of a Lady . . . a real one, who after the death of her husband lived alone in a vast mansion and had these served for tea daily from Monday to Friday but, poor soul, never ate one herself. . . . Patés and terrines are really very simple to make but often suffer from over-cooking when made at home. Follow the recipe and remember to keep them in the refrigerator after allowing them to cool and they should give you no trouble. Home-made ones are not that difficult and are much more delicious than the supermarket varieties.

Not everyone would conceive of the mushroom as a starter vegetable but the recipes provided here do in fact set the mushroom in a very good and flavoursome light provided they are fresh and firm before you start cooking them. Never reheat mushroom dishes as this does ruin the flavour.

The *Stilton dip* I cannot resist. It is one of those dishes that breaks down barriers almost straight away when served with a large plate of chunky uncooked vegetables in the middle of the table. When everyone has to dive in together, social restraint has to go! I was in one of the poorer quarters of Paris when I first had this dish and much to my surprise the combinations of the raw vegetables with a similar dip, but not Stilton, was quite delicious. As well as carrots and cucumber you can use raw cauliflower florets, broccoli, radishes and celery, and of course, nuts and savoury biscuits.

# Cream of lettuce soup

1 large lettuce, roughly shredded
1 large onion, chopped
½ pint of single cream (275 ml)
2 ozs butter (50 g)
1 pint of well-seasoned chicken stock (570 ml)

In a large flame-proof casserole, melt the butter
gently adding the lettuce and onion and cooking
very, very gently for about fifteen minutes, until
they are softened but not browned.

Add the chicken stock, bring to the boil and
simmer for a further ten minutes. Allow to cool
slightly before liquidising the soup in a food
processor. Return the liquid to the casserole and
add the cream, increasing the heat gradually until
it is just comes up to the boil. Serve at once.

This soup looks attractive garnished with a very
thin slice of cucumber, sprinkled with paprika.

# Artichoke soup

8 ozs onions (225 g)
2 ozs butter (50 g)
12 ozs Jerusalem artichokes (350 g)
8 ozs potatoes (225 g)
1 pint of chicken stock (570 ml)
1 level tablespoon plain flour
1 pint of milk (570 ml)
3 ozs smoked streaky bacon (75 g)
salt and black pepper
¼ pint of single cream (150 ml)

Chop the onions finely, peel the artichokes and
potatoes and cut them into cubes.

Melt the butter in a thick saucepan and add the
onion and sweat until it is soft (about ten to
fifteen minutes). Remove the saucepan from the
heat.

Add the potatoes and artichokes to the
saucepan and continue to fry very gently for a
further fifteen minutes, stirring all the time.

Pour in the stock and cook for twenty to thirty
minutes at a simmer. Sieve or liquidise the soup
in a food processor to make a puree, and return
this to the saucepan. Blend the flour with a little
of the milk to make a roux and mix this into the
puree. Add the rest of the milk and bring to the
boil. Simmer for five minutes. Meanwhile, cut the
bacon into little strips and fry until crisp. Drain
the bacon of all fat and reserve for garnishing.

Season the soup to taste with salt and pepper,

and just before serving swirl in the cream and scatter on the crispy bacon pieces.

Delicious served with hot, buttered, crusty rolls.

# Celery and leek soup

2lb fresh leeks (900 g)
1 head of celery
1 large onion
1½ pints of chicken stock (845 ml)
bay leaf
1 tablespoon chopped parsley
salt and black pepper
2 ozs butter (50 g)

Wash all the vegetables well and finely chop them together. A food processor is ideal for this. Melt the butter in the thickest saucepan that you have and gently, indeed very gently, sauté the vegetables for about fifteen to twenty minutes until they are well and truly soft. Add the bay leaf, the parsley and the stock and simmer very gently for one-and-a-half hours. Adjust the seasoning and serve with fresh brown rolls.

This soup can be frozen without ruining it and can be made for strict vegetarians using alternatives to butter and vegetable instead of chicken stock.

# Crevettes au Fromage

6 ozs cooked prawns (175 g)
4 ozs Philadelphia cheese (110 g)
1 small Boursin cheese
1 15 ozs tin condensed consomme soup
  (450 ml)
salt and black pepper

Cream together the cheeses and then add the cold
consomme soup, blending thoroughly. Season
with a little salt and pepper and then gently fold
in the prawns. Place the mixture in individual
ramekins and allow to set in a chilled place,
preferably a refrigerator. This will take about
twelve hours so these are best cooked (or should
I say combined) the day before, and left
overnight.

Decorate with a twist of lemon and serve with
thinly sliced brown bread and butter.

# Miniature quiches

Pastry:

      1 lb self-raising flour (450 g)
      ½ teaspoon salt
      8 ozs Gouda cheese (grated) (225 g)
      8 ozs butter (225 g)
      1 egg, beaten
      a little cold water

Filling:

      3 eggs, beaten
      ½ pint of single cream (275 ml)
      salt and black pepper
      2 tablespoons sweetcorn
      6 ozs smoked haddock, cooked and
         flaked (175 g)
      6 ozs smoked gammon, cooked and
         chopped (175 g)
      1 tablespoon chopped parsley

Nothing about this delicious starter or picnic dish is difficult to achieve. Start with the pastry. Sift together the flour and the salt and stir in the grated cheese. Rub in the butter until the mixture resembles breadcrumbs and then add the beaten egg and the water if necessary. Work together lightly to form a dough and leave the ball of pastry in a cool place until you are ready to use it.

    The fillings are very simple. Mix together the eggs and cream, salt and pepper and sweetcorn and divide into two bowls. In one bowl add the flaked fish in the other bowl the gammon. Keep the parsley for decoration.

Roll out the pastry and line about twelve individual quiche tins or ramekins with it. Divide the fillings between the pastry cases.

Bake for thirty-five minutes on a metal baking tray in an oven preheated to 400 f, Gas 6, 200 c.

Sprinkle with chopped parsley and serve warm.

# Sardine savouries

12 fresh or frozen sardines
8 ozs cooked potatoes mashed with butter, a
    tablespoon of chopped onion, an egg, a
    little cream, salt and black pepper and a
    pinch of mixed herbs, preferably L'Herbes
    de Provence
1 tablespoon olive oil

Frozen sardines are now widely available and are
delicious. The trick is to remove as many of the
bones as possible before using them. For this you
really need a very sharp knife. Slit the sardine
down the back from the rear of the head to the
base of the tail fins, and not (as traditionally)
through the belly. Then with a little care and a
nimble finger you can pull out the back bone
and most of the fine bones.

To make the mashed potato mixture it is best
to use a food processor or a blender into which
you can put all the ingredients at once. The best
herbs for this dish are L'Herbes de Provence
which are now widely available from shops. Blend
the potato mixture well.

With the oil, thinly cover a baking tray and lay
the sardines on it belly down with the split facing
upwards so that this can be filled with the potato
mixture. The best way to do this is with a piping
bag and a suitable nozzle.

Pre-heat the oven to 325 f, Gas 3, 170 c and
bake for about twenty-five minutes.

This is a very tasty and surprisingly good starter. Three sardines per person is quite enough usually.

# Liver paté

12 ozs pig's liver (350 g)
12 ozs streaky bacon (350 g)
1 small onion, finely chopped
1 small egg
1 garlic clove, chopped
salt and black pepper
½ teaspoon ground mace
1 oz butter (25 g)
1 glass of sweet sherry

Gently melt the butter in a thick frying pan and add the finely chopped onion and garlic and cook until soft but not brown. Remove from the heat.

Wash the liver and cut into small pieces, or if you have a mincer do use that. Remove the rind from the bacon and set aside four rashers before coarsely mincing the rest.

Place all the ingredients except the reserved rashers of bacon in a large mixing bowl and stir well. Leave to stand for about an hour.

In the meantime grease a 2 lb (900 g) loaf tin with a little butter and line it with the bacon slices reserved. Put the paté mixture in the tin, pressing it down well, and cover it with foil. Place in the centre of the oven set at 350 f, Gas 4, 180 c and cook for an hour and forty-five minutes.

Allow to cool before chilling and serve with hot toasted granary bread. Truly tasty!

# Chicken and sausagemeat terrine

12 ozs pork sausagemeat (350 g)
6 ozs boneless breast, skin removed (175 g)
4 ozs smoked streaky bacon (110 g)
1 medium onion
1 teaspoon dried sage
1 bay leaf
1 oz butter (25 g)

Finely chop the onion and mix with the sausagemeat and sage and leave to one side. With a very sharp knife slice the skinned chicken breasts lengthways into half-inch wide strips.

Line a 1 lb (450 g) loaf tin with the butter and bacon and bay leaf and put in a third of the sausagemeat mixture and then a layer of the chicken. Repeat this and add a final layer of sausagemeat.

Wrap the tin in foil and place in a roasting dish half-filled with water and cook in the centre of the oven at 375 f, Gas 5, 190 c for an hour. Allow to cool. Then chill thoroughly before turning it out on to a serving dish.

This is a delicious starter for those who like terrines but are not friends of the garlic! Excellent with toast.

# Sardine paté

6 ozs Philadelphia cheese (175 g)
4 ozs sardines in oil (110 g)
1 dessertspoon fresh parsley
1 teaspoon fresh thyme
the greated rind and juice of half a lemon

For this tasty paté, the method is very simple.
Mix all the ingredients together with a fork apart
from the lemon. Then squeeze in the lemon juice
and add some of the finely grated rind. Place in
a dish and chill well before serving.

This paté can be made just as successfully in a
food processor.

Serve with thin slices of toast and butter.

# Button mushroom bake

1 lb button mushrooms (450 g)
4 ozs butter (110 g)
1 large garlic clove
1 lemon
½ pint of double cream (675 ml)
chopped parsley

Wipe the mushrooms with a damp cloth and
remove the stalks and reserve for a soup or
something. Place the mushrooms underside up on
a shallow baking dish and sprinkle with the juice
of the lemon. Finely chop the garlic clove and
blend with the butter and then, using two
teaspoons, place a knob of the garlic butter into
each of the mushroom caps. Pour over the cream
and bake in the oven at 400 f, Gas 6, or 200 c for
thirty minutes.

Sprinkle with chopped parsley and serve piping
hot with fresh brown bread and butter.

# Stuffed button mushrooms

6 button mushrooms per person (175 g)
6 ozs liver paté (175 g)
3 ozs chopped walnuts (75 g)
1 egg, beaten
6 ozs breadcrumbs (175 g)
salt and black pepper

Wash the mushrooms and remove the stalks.

Chop up the walnuts and mushrooms stalks and blend together with the paté, half the egg mixture and 2 ozs of the breadcrumbs. Season with salt and black pepper.

Stuff each mushroom with this mixture and coat them in the remaining egg before rolling in the rest of the breadcrumbs.

Deep fry the mushrooms for one minute or if you prefer, shallow fry them in lots of butter for about three minutes and serve with a squeeze of lemon juice.

Delicious with fresh crispy rolls and lots of butter.

# Stilton dip

6 ozs ripe Stilton cheese, grated (175 g)
6 ozs cottage cheese (175 g)
5 ozs carton of single cream (150 ml)
2 teaspoons freshly chopped parsley
1 teaspoon Worcestershire sauce
1 teaspoon paprika
3 drops of Tabasco sauce

This is a very tangy dish and is especially good before a robust main course, of lamb especially. Simply blend all the ingredients together in a food processor or liquidiser and place in a stoneware dish. Cover and chill for a few hours.

To serve, take a selection of carrots, celery, cucumber and apple cut into chunks and allow everyone to dip in, passing the bowl around.

# Family · Feasting

# FISH

'We remember the fish we did eat . . .'
*Numbers Chapter Eleven*

A selection of interesting dishes with fish and
other fruits of the sea.

## RECIPES:

*Abbot Arnold's pancake*
*Kedgeree*
*Tuna fish spaghetti*
*Haddock à l'orange*
*Fisherman's pancakes*
*Russian fish pie*
*Pilgrim's fish pie*
*Devonshire cod*
*Mussels Provençal*
*Seafood ring*

It is funny how fish and Christianity seem to go hand in hand, or should I say fin in fin?? Was it really our Lord's thumbprint on the haddock? Well it certainly is a good story and in early Christianity the fish was a secret sign among believers. The Greek word for fish, I C T H U S, was used as a mnemonic:

| I | Iesous | (Jesus – I in Greek being the same as J) |
|---|---|---|
| Ch | Christos | (Christ) |
| Th | Theou | (God's) |
| U | Uios | (Son) |
| S | Soter | (Saviour) |

And so the symbol of the fish came to be used as an expression of this truth. Once unravelled the sign carries a wealth of meaning. It was often used on tombstones of the second and third centuries.

I have had some fun with one or two recipes in this book and *Abbot Arnold's pancake* is one of them . . . Arnold never was an Abbot but was so pious a churchwarden that his children thought he deserved the title.

*Kedgeree* is perhaps (and hopefully) coming into vogue again and not just for breakfast. I hope it does, as in fact it makes a very good and cheap meal, full of flavour. I sometimes cook the rice in some fish stock if I have any, and it certainly makes a difference.

The thing to remember is that you can almost use any white fish for these dishes i.e. cod instead of plaice, haddock instead of halibut, depending upon your pocket. Remember too that fish is supposed to be very good for the grey matter! Has the decline in the fish industry in this country also meant a decline in our brain power? I wonder.

*Mussels Provençal* and *Seafood ring* are a couple of recipes I have adapted from my trips to the South of France where you can get the most delicious seafoods. In fact, you can even see them swimming in the harbours, they are so plentiful.

Mussels are not everyone's choice, but along with oysters used to be the staple diet of many poor people in this country in the 17th century. In recent years they have become the subject of commercial cultivation and fresh ones are widely available. You can obtain them cooked and frozen but I often wonder why the manufacturers bother to do this, as the fresh ones are so superior and are much more popular.

# Abbot Arnold's pancake

1 large tin of salmon
1 lb hot cooked potatoes (450 g)
2 ozs butter (50 g)
2 tablespoons soured cream
salt and black pepper
1 tablespoon tarragon vinegar
2 eggs, beaten separately
4 ozs dried breadcrumbs (110 g)
2 ozs butter (50 g)
chopped parsley

Mash together the salmon and the hot potatoes together with the butter, soured cream and tarragon vinegar, and finally one of the beaten eggs. Allow to stand for a time to firm up but if it seems a little runny add some more potato.

In a large frying pan, melt one ounce of butter and carefully form a large 'pancake' with the fish and potato mixture, keeping it over a low heat.

Paint the upper side of the 'pancake' with the other beaten egg and sprinkle with the breadcrumbs. When you feel the under side is cooked a little turn the pancake out by placing a cutting board on top of the pan and flipping it over out on to the board. Heat a little more butter and then carefully slide the pancake back in the pan and breaded side down. Fry gently for a further five minutes or so. Turn the pancake out on to a board or plate and serve cut in wedges.

If you prefer you can make small individual 'cakes' which, unlike abbots in the past, are less troublesome to manage!

# Kedgeree

1 lb smoked haddock (450 g)
1 small onion, finely chopped
6 ozs long grained rice (175 g)
2 hard boiled eggs
1 bay leaf
1 oz butter (25 g)
salt
cayenne pepper
chopped parsley for garnishing
1 slice of lemon

Cut the haddock into smallish pieces, place in a pan and cover with cold water. Bring this to the boil and then remove from the heat and allow to stand.

Cook the rice with the bay leaf, lemon slice and salt in plenty of water.

Meanwhile, heat the butter in a frying pan and gently fry the onion until it is soft.

Drain the rice and place it in a warmed dish and stir in the onion and the flaked fish. Quarter the eggs and arrange them on the top of the kedgeree and decorate with chopped parsley and cayenne pepper.

# Tuna fish spaghetti

1 6 oz tin tuna fish, drained and flaked (175 g)
1 15 ozs can of chicken soup (450 ml)
2 ozs butter (50 g)
4 ozs mushrooms, washed and sliced (110 g)
1 garlic clove, finely chopped
salt and black pepper
1 tablespoon vegetable oil
3 tablespoons dry sherry
1 lb spaghetti (450 g)

Cook the spaghetti as directed on the packet.

*For the sauce:*
Melt the butter and the oil in a thick saucepan
and gently fry the garlic and sliced mushrooms.
Remove from the heat and stir in the chicken soup
and the sherry. Heat through thoroughly and
then add the flaked tuna fish. Adjust seasoning to
taste.

Strain the cooked spaghetti and place on a large
serving dish. Pour over the sauce and sprinkle
with chopped parsley.

Serve at once.

# Haddock à l'orange

1 lb haddock (450 g)
5 fl ozs concentrated frozen orange juice
  (150 ml)
The grated rind of one orange
1 clove garlic, finely chopped
2 ozs butter (50 g)
salt and black pepper

Divide the haddock into four portions and set
aside. Melt the butter gently in a frying pan and
add the grated rind of the orange and the
breadcrumbs, together with the finely chopped
garlic. Cook until the butter is absorbed by the
breadcrumbs and the whole mixture is fairly
crumbly.

Place the portions of fish in a buttered serving
dish and spread the breadcrumbs mixture over
the top and pour over the orange juice.

Bake in an oven uncovered for twenty to thirty
minutes at 375 f, Gas 5, 190 c.

A delicious dish for the spring, served with new
potatoes and garden peas.

# Fisherman's pancakes

Batter:

>    4 ozs wheatmeal flour (110 g)
>    ½ pint of milk (275 ml)
>    1 egg
>    salt
>    1 tablespoon oil

Filling:

>    12 ozs cooked white or smoked fish,
>       flaked (350 g)
>    grated rind and juice of a lemon
>    ¼ pint of double cream (150 ml)
>    2 ozs white breadcrumbs (50 g)
>    2 ozs Gruyere cheese, grated (50 g)
>    1 tablespoon chopped parsley
>    1 egg

Blend together the ingredients for the batter in a food processor and leave to stand in a cool place for at least an hour.

For the filling, beat the egg into the cream. Add the flaked fish, the grated lemon rind and lemon juice, gently folding all the ingredients together.

Make eight pancakes with the batter and divide the fish mixture between them. Roll them up and place them in an oven-proof dish. Sprinkle on to the pancakes a mixture of the breadcrumbs and the grated Gruyere cheese. Dot with a little butter and brown under a hot grill for ten minutes or so.

Serve immediately.

# Russian fish pie

8 ozs puff pastry (frozen will do) (225 g)
1 lb filleted plaice, uncooked (450 g)
1 teaspoon chopped parsley
½ teaspoon pepper
1 teaspoon finely grated lemon rind
½ teaspoon salt
1 hardboiled egg, cut in quarters
1 raw egg
The juice of one lemon

Roll the pastry into a largish square, remembering never to turn the pastry over!

Cut the raw fish into inch-sized squares and place in the centre of the pastry. Sprinkle on the parsley, pepper, lemon rind, salt and juice of the lemon.

Fold the corners of the pastry into the centre to make a parcel and seal the edges with the beaten raw egg. If there are scraps of pastry left over, use these to decorate the 'parcel' in any way that you think fit and brush over with the raw egg.

Place on a baking tray in the centre of a hot oven 425 f, Gas 7, 220 c, for about twenty-five minutes.

Serve garnished with the hardboiled egg.

This goes well with a salad.

# Pilgrims' fish pie

This dish is for a *large* family . . . or a horde of hungry students (or pilgrims, if any are passing your way!) It is said that this once fed fifteen hungry pilgrims on their way to Iona from Durham. I guess they kept to the coastal route, hence a ready supply of fish. There are many recipes for fish pies, but this one made in this large quantity is a good standby if you unexpectedly find yourself host to the visiting rugby team (who will not go away hungry when served with this dish).

3 lbs white fish, cod or coley will do well
   (1 kg 350 g)
8 ozs packet frozen mixed vegetables, thawed
   (225 g)
1 lb onions (450 g)
2 large cans of tomatoes
1 15 ozs can of sweetcorn (425 g)
1 dessertspoon mixed herbs
salt and black pepper
3 pints of white sauce (1 litre 710 ml) made
   from:
     3 ozs butter (75 g)
     3 ozs plain flour (75 g)
     3 pints of milk (1 litre 710 ml)
6 lb old potatoes (2 kg 700 g)
8 ozs grated cheddar cheese (225 g)
½ pint of milk (275 ml)
1 bay leaf

Skin and bone the fish as well as possible. Place in a baking dish with the bay leaf and a little salt and pepper and pour on the half pint of milk. Cover and bake in the oven at 350 f, Gas 4, 180 c for about twenty minutes until it is cooked. When it is cooked, flake the fish into a large bowl.

Cook the potatoes in the usual way by boiling with a little salt, and mash them with a little butter and the grated cheese.

Chop the onions and gently soften in a little of the butter in a large, thick saucepan. When they are soft, add the rest of the butter and the flour to form a roux and gradually stir in the milk, beating well, until a thick sauce is formed. Add the frozen vegetables and the can of sweetcorn together with the tomatoes and then fold in the flaked fish. Adjust the seasoning and add the herbs. When everything is mixed well place in a large oven-proof dish and spread over the mashed potatoes.

Put in an oven at 375 f, Gas 5, 190 c, and cook for thirty-five minutes.

Serve piping hot.

# Devonshire cod

1 lb cod (450 g)
half a pint of dry cider (275 ml)
1 oz butter (25 g)
salt and black pepper to taste
1 tomato
2 ozs mushrooms (50 g)
½ oz flour (10 g)
½ oz butter (10 g)
chopped parsley for garnishing

Cut the cod into one inch cubes and place in a baking dish. Skin and chop up the tomato with the mushrooms and sprinkle on to the fish. Cover with the cider and dot with the ounce of butter and pop in the oven for about thirty minutes at 375 f, Gas 5, 190 c. Strain off the cooking liquid into a jug or bowl and keep the fish warm.

In a small thick saucepan melt the half ounce of butter and add the flour to form a roux. Gradually add the liquid from the cooked fish and make a thickish sauce. Season it with salt and pepper. Pour the sauce over the fish and pop back in the oven for ten minutes.

Sprinkle with parsley and serve with piped mashed potatoes.

# Mussels provençal

Allow about 18 mussels per person

4 ozs butter (110 g)
3 garlic cloves, chopped
salt
2 ozs breadcrumbs (50 g)
1 oz parsley (25 g)
¼ teaspoon each of thyme, marjoram, basil
black pepper
1 tablespoon oatmeal

Soak the mussels in water with the tablespoon of oatmeal and then scrub well.

Place them on a large baking tray and fire under a very hot grill until they open. Discard those which do not open.

In a bowl mix together the butter, chopped garlic and the rest of the ingredients. Then spoon this paste on each mussel, place back on the baking tray and fire them in a hot oven for fifteen minutes.

Enjoy them with lots of butter and hot crusty bread.

# Seafood ring

8 ozs scallops (225 g)
8 ozs cod, skinned and cut into inch-sized
    cubes (225 g)
6 ozs prawns, peeled (175 g)
4 ozs mushrooms (110 g)
3 ozs butter (75 g)
3 fl ozs dry sherry (75 ml)
1 medium sized onion, chopped
1 lb tomatoes, peeled, deseeded and chopped
    (450 g)
2 level teaspoons tomato puree
1 teaspoon Herbs of Provence
2 level teaspoons cornflour
1 garlic clove, crushed
½ lemon

For the rice:
        1 oz butter (25 g)
        12 ozs long grain rice (350 g)
        1½ pints of water (845 ml)
        1 onion, finely chopped
        2 level teaspoons salt

To prepare the rice, melt the butter in a thick
saucepan and add the finely chopped onion and
cook until it is soft but not brown. Add the rice
and stir for a couple of minutes before adding
the salt and water. Cover with a close fitting lid
and cook for twenty minutes stirring
occasionally. Drain and rinse the rice under cold

running water. Pack the rice into a greased ten-inch (25.5 cm) ring mould and smooth the top. Place in the refrigerator for one hour.

## The Fish Filling

Melt one ounce of butter in a pan and gently fry the chopped onion and crushed garlic until they are soft and then add in the sliced mushrooms and cook for a further three minutes. Add the prepared tomatoes and the tomato puree together with the herbs.

Blend together a little of the sherry with the cornflour and add this to the tomato and onion mixture, together with the lemon juice and finally the rest of the sherry. Turn the heat down and allow to simmer for twenty minutes or so.

Adjust the seasoning to taste.

In a frying pan heat the remaining butter and gently fry the fish and the scallops for ten to fifteen minutes. Add these to the tomato mixture and allow to cool.

Turn the rice ring out onto a serving dish and fill the centre with the cooled fish mixture and decorate with the prawns.

A delicious dish for a summer buffet.

# Family · Feasting

# POULTRY

'And if the burnt sacrifice be fowls . . .'
*Leviticus Chapter One*

Chicken is now the second most popular meat
in Britain and one of my favourites, but
traditionally other birds of the air were
enjoyed as well, but the chicken is a versatile
bird and so economical.

## *RECIPES:*

*A quick chicken casserole*
*Chicken divan*
*Citrus chicken*
*Barbecued chicken with fruit*
*The Three Kings favourite chicken dish*
*Sere Joseph Marie's Normandy chicken*
*Hungarian paprika chicken*
*Turkey legs in red wine sauce*
*Rachel's sinful chicken*
*Chicken and walnuts*

I have a very simple rule for cooking chicken tastily: buy a chilled fresh one rather than a frozen one. I cannot stand the frozen kind.

For a good, flavoursome roast, take a medium sized onion and peel it, and place it in the abdominal cavity of the chicken, placing any fat that may be in the bird on top of it. Rub the chicken with a little oil and sprinkle with a liberal coating of black pepper and salt, dot with a little butter and roast in the oven at 375 f, Gas 5, 190 c, for twenty minutes per pound and fifteen minutes over.

But not everyone likes their chicken that way, and when you cannot always obtain the sort of bird that you would like, it is a good idea to dress it up a bit before serving it. So here are some recipes that may tempt you a little but will not be too difficult for the busy cook to achieve.

A recipe for turkey legs has crept in and this is no bad thing as I do find that there are lots of them around, and usually they need some cooking attention to make them worthwhile. . . .

# A quick chicken casserole

4 chicken joints
1 onion, finely chopped
2 tablespoons olive oil
1 garlic clove, chopped
1 15 ozs tin chopped tomatoes (425 g)
6 ozs smoked streaky bacon, cut in strips and
    fried (175 g)
1 teaspoon Italian seasoning
1 teaspoon Worcestershire sauce
1 chicken stock cube
salt and black pepper

In a small casserole heat the oil and fry the onion
until soft. Add the chopped garlic to the onion
along with some salt and black pepper and cook
for a further minute. Add the chicken joints, the
tinned tomatoes, herbs, Worcestershire sauce and
the bacon pieces. Finally crumble in the stock
cube.

Check the seasoning and bring to the boil
before covering and popping in the oven set at
375 f, Gas 5, 190 c. Bake for forty-five minutes.

Serve with chunks of crispy fried bread.

# Chicken divan

4 boned chicken breasts
1 lb broccoli (450 g)
¼ pint of mayonnaise (150 ml)
1 can of condensed chicken soup
2 teaspoons curry paste
½ lb button mushrooms, sliced (225 g)
1 glass of cream sherry
2 ozs of breadcrumbs (50 g)
2 ozs of grated Cheddar or Gruyere cheese
   (50 g)
2 tablespoons vegetable oil
salt and black pepper
Butter for frying

Oil a baking tray and place on it the chicken
breasts sprinkled with a little salt and lots of
black pepper. Cook for twenty minutes at 375 f,
Gas 5, 190 c. Cook the broccoli in lightly salted
water until tender.

In a thick saucepan melt the butter and gently
fry the sliced mushrooms for a couple of
minutes. Add the mayonnaise, soup, curry paste,
and the sherry and heat through gently.

Butter a deep oven dish and arrange the strained
cooked broccoli on the bottom. Lay the chicken
breasts on the broccoli and pour over the sauce.
Sprinkle over the breadcrumbs and grated cheese.

Bake in an oven at 350 f, Gas 4, 180 c, for
thirty to forty minutes.

Serve unaccompanied – a delicious all-in-one dish.

# Citrus chicken

4 chicken breasts
2 lemons
2 limes
rind of 1 lemon
1 teaspoon thyme
½ teaspoon fresh parsley, chopped
2 ozs butter (50 g)
½ oz cornflour (10 g)
1 glass of dry sherry
salt and black pepper

In a deep dish, make a marinade using the juice of the lemons and limes, the lemon rind (ensure first that all pith is removed) and the herbs. Put the chicken breasts into this, spooning over the citrus mixture. Cover the dish and leave to marinate in a refrigerator for about four hours.

Lightly grease a shallow baking dish and place the chicken joints in the dish along with the marinade. Add the sherry. Cover and cook for about forty minutes in an oven set at 350 f, Gas 4, 180 c.

When the breasts are lightly cooked remove them from dish and keep warm. Blend together the butter and cornflour and add to the delicious sauce to thicken it. Pour the sauce over the hot chicken.

# Barbecued chicken with fruit

This is an extra-special dish to serve at well-organised barbecue parties! It may be a little ambitious for scout camps!

1 chicken weighing about 3½ lbs, ready for stuffing (1 kg 575 g)

Stuffing:
>           2 small onions or 1 large one
>           2 tablespoons sultanas
>           2 tablespoons currants
>           1 lime
>           salt and pepper
>           1 clove

½ cup of lemon juice
½ cup of tomato juice
a pinch of saffron
6 ozs butter (175 g)
2 tablespoons olive oil

Chop up the onion and the lime coarsely, mix with the dried fruit and add the clove. Sprinkle a little salt and black pepper inside the chicken and fill with the stuffing. Sew up the cavity or secure with a skewer.

Place the chicken in a large casserole dish.

Add to the casserole dish the lemon and tomato juices and the saffron. Cover and cook in a moderate oven 350 f, Gas 4, 180 c, until the bird begins to tenderise (about forty-five minutes).

Melt the butter and oil together. Remove the bird from the casserole and place on two large skewers and finish cooking over blazing charcoal remembering to baste liberally with the oil and butter mixture.

Serve with a green salad and baked jacket potatoes.

# The Three Kings favourite chicken dish

Another barbecue special.

4 chicken joints, preferably legs
1 small onion
¼ pint of water (150 ml)
½ teaspoon peppercorns
½ cup of lemon juice
2 large firm tomatoes
4 ozs butter (110 g)

Place the chicken joints in a large pan with the water, lemon juice, chopped onion, peppercorns and the large tomatoes sliced up on top. Cover them and bake them in a moderate oven 350 f, Gas 4, 180 c, until the joints are tender but not falling apart (about twenty-five minutes).

Remove the joints from the pan and carefully place them on skewers and baste them well with masses of melted butter before firing over the charcoal grill turning frequently until they are golden brown.

Serve them immediately with a fresh salad of crisp lettuce and sliced green peppers.

Do make sure that you do not overcook the chicken joints as this will spoil the dish.

# Sere Joseph Marie's Normandy chicken

At one end of a village there are nuns, and at the other end of the same village there are monks. At around 4 p.m., when I think it is time for Vespers (not the two wheeled variety) a 'NUNMOBILE' full of flowing habits can be seen rushing towards the Abbey of Le Bec Hellouin where both communities get together to offer Divine Worship.

Hospitality plays an important part in any religious house, and the monks and nuns of Le Bec Hellouin are no exception. In fact they positively delight in their guests, albeit rather quietly and they have often entertained me royally. However as the seasoned pilgrim to Le Bec will soon come to understand that the nuns are the better cooks, hence this dish . . . there are rather a lot of cans around the monks' kitchen!!

4 chicken joints, preferably legs
1 large onion
1 oz butter (25 g)
1 dessertspoon plain flour
2 medium sized leeks
½ pint of medium cider (275 ml)
salt and black pepper
1 chicken stock cube

Melt the butter in a casserole and brown the chicken joints. Remove from the pan.

Chop up the onion and the leeks and add to the pan and cook until they are softened but not brown. Stir in the flour and cook for a minute before gradually adding the cider. Crumble in the stock cube and season with some salt and black pepper. Cook until the sauce begins to thicken and then return the joints.

Cover the dish and place in a moderate oven 350 f, Gas 4, 180 c, and bake for forty minutes or until the chicken joints are cooked.

Serve with plain boiled rice or mashed potatoes.

# Hungarian paprika chicken

1 3½ lb chicken, or four chicken pieces (1 kg 575 g)
salt and black pepper
1 tablespoon paprika
1 medium sized onion, chopped
2 ozs butter (50 g)
3 tablespoons double cream
3 tablespoons paprika
1 pint of chicken stock (570 ml)
2 ozs plain flour (50 g)
6 tablespoons water
1 lemon
¼ pint of white wine (150 ml)

Take an ounce of flour and season it with the salt and black pepper. Joint the chicken and roll the pieces in the seasoned flour. In a thick casserole melt half the butter and brown the chicken joints all over and remove from the dish. Add the rest of the butter and soften the chopped onion in it. When the onion is transparent add the rest of the flour and the paprika and cook for a minute stirring it all together. Gradually add the chicken stock along with the water. Cook until the sauce thickens and then put the chicken joints back in the casserole again. Place in a moderate oven 350 f, Gas 4, 180 c, and cook for about forty minutes. Remove the chicken joints on to a serving dish and keep them warm. Then to the sauce add the cream, lemon juice and a slosh of white wine. Heat through thoroughly and pour over the chicken.

Excellent with noodles.

# Turkey legs in red wine sauce

2 large turkey legs
3 tablespoons oil
1 medium onion
6 ozs button mushrooms (175 g)
½ pint beef stock (275 ml)
1 cup of red wine
1 tablespoon flour
½ cup of milk
salt and black pepper
thyme
1 dessertspoon paprika

Heat the oil in a thick casserole and toss in some salt, black pepper and about a teaspoonful of thyme. Brown the turkey legs in this and then set to one side. Chop the onion and cook gently in the oil before adding the sliced mushrooms. Sprinkle on the flour and gently add the stock and red wine. As the sauce begins to thicken, add the milk and paprika to taste, and adjust the seasoning. Put the joints back into the casserole and cover. Place in a moderate oven 350 f, Gas 4, 180 c, and cook for about forty-five minutes until the joints are tender.

Serve with plain boiled rice.

# Rachel's sinful chicken

eight chicken joints
salt and black pepper
1 medium onion, sliced
1 large carrot, sliced
1 bay leaf
2 sprigs of parsley
3 ozs butter (75 g)
3 ozs plain flour (75 g)
5 fl ozs double cream (150 ml)
5 fl ozs single cream (150 ml)
1 measure of dry sherry
½ ozs flaked almonds (10 g)
8 ozs button mushrooms (225 g)
6 ozs breadcrumbs (175 g)
3 ozs extra butter (75 g)

In a large casserole place the chicken joints along
with the sliced onion, carrot and bay leaf and
the sprigs of parsley. Cover with water and bring
to the boil and allow to simmer for about an
hour-and-a-half. Lift out the chicken joints and
remove the meat from the bones leaving as much
as possible in large chunks. Strain the stock and
reserve. In a large saucepan melt the butter, blend
in the flour and cook for three or four minutes
over a low heat. Then blend in the sherry, and
the creams together with half a pint (or a little
less) of the stock. Stir the sauce and allow it to
thicken somewhat before adding the sliced
mushrooms and almonds.

Place the chicken meat in a shallow baking dish and cover with the sauce. Cover well with the breadcrumbs and dot well with the three ounces of butter and bake in the oven at 250 f, Gas ½, 130 c for thirty to forty minutes until golden brown.

Serve immediately with rice.

# Chicken and walnuts

1½ lb of uncooked chicken meat, cut into
   one-inch cubes (700 g)
6 ozs chopped walnuts (175 g)
2 ozs chopped stem ginger (50 g)
2 tablespoons soy sauce
1 glass of dry sherry
2 tablespoons cornflour
½ pint of chicken stock (275 ml)
1 egg white
½ pint of corn oil (275 ml)
1 teaspoon cornflour
1 garlic clove, crushed

If you have a wok it is ideal for this dish, but if
not do not rush out and buy one, a frying pan
will do!

Drench the chicken pieces in the egg white
before tossing them in the two tablespoons of
cornflour.

In the wok or frying pan pour nearly a cupful
of oil and heat. Fry the walnuts in this for half
a minute to flavour the oil and remove them to a
warm dish. Do the same with the ginger,
allowing it to fry for a few minutes. Remove and
place with the walnuts. Take a few chunks of the
chicken at a time and cook in the oil until they
turn pale-gold in colour. Set them to one side in
a warm dish. Add the clove of crushed garlic to
the oil mixture, together with the soy sauce and
the sherry and cook for a couple of minutes before

adding the cornflour mixed with the chicken
stock. Cook until the sauce begins to thicken. Stir
in the walnuts and ginger and finally the chicken.

You have now a delicious dish to serve with
rice.

# Family · Feasting

# BEEF

'And Adam gave names to all the cattle . . .'

*Genesis Chapter Two*

(Eve, however, did not manage all the recipes!)

## *RECIPES:*

*Shepherd's pie*
*Hungarian goulash*
*Beef Liege*
*Beef stroganoff*
*Meat loaf*
*Flemish carbonade*
*Beef casserole with savoury dumplings*
*Veronique's (or Patrick's) chouchouka*
*Chili beef*
*Braised oxtail*

One glorious summer I had young people from all over staying at the vicarage. It was not some holy convention but just a group of friends who had converged upon us all at the same time. It was great fun and they took turns in doing the odd bit of cooking, and, mercifully, the washing up. I never knew what sort of meal I was going to come home to in the evening, but it was never a disappointment.

Although our tastes differed, we did all lament the price of one of our favourite meats and that, of course, was beef. However between us, we did manage to produce from the cheaper cuts some tasty and internationally-flavoured meals.

With the more economical cuts, of course, slower cooking is essential for good results and that has always been acknowledged among cooks. The problem always is knowing for how long and at what temperature we should cook them. This isn't made any easier as everyone's oven seems to be temperamentally different! If it is any comfort, I believe that it is quite hard to *overcook* some of the tougher portions of beef and a deliciously satisfying meal can be reaped from some of the cheapest cuts.

I do think it is worth investing in a couple of really good quality casserole dishes that hold the heat and can be used in all sorts of ovens.

Our guest Veronique scored a hit with her *Chouchouka* although I believe it was her fiancé Patrick who really did all the cooking! But then she was a very charming person and no-one would have doubted her word. Patrick remained loyally silent throughout all the questioning on the technicalities of the recipe.

# Shepherd's pie

1 lb potatoes (450 g)
1 lb minced beef (450 g)
2 tablespoons oil
1 medium sized onion, chopped
1 small green pepper, chopped
1 small red pepper, chopped
1 carrot, chopped
butter
salt and black pepper

Peel and dice the potatoes and cook them gently until almost done. Strain off the water and stand them to one side.

In a thick saucepan heat the oil and brown the meat well. Remove from the pan and set to one side. In the same pan fry all the other vegetables for a few minutes. Leave the lid on, but remember to stir the pan occasionally. You may need a little more oil for this.

After about five minutes, add the mince and mix well with the vegetables, adjusting the seasoning as required. There should be enough moisture to make a good lot of juice but if preferred you can add a little stock. Not too much, mind.

Place the meat mixture in a deep pie dish and cover the lot with the diced potato and dot it well with butter. Pop it in the oven set at gas mark 6, 400 f, 200 c, and cook for twenty-five minutes.

This pie should delight any shepherd. I should know – my father was one.

# Hungarian goulash

1½ lb lean stewing or braising beef (700 g)
1 lb onions sliced (450 g)
2 ozs beef dripping (50 g)
1 garlic clove
1 level tablespoon paprika
1 level tablespoon plain flour
salt
black pepper
½ pint of stock (275 ml)
1 level teaspoon caraway seeds
2 tablespoons soured cream

Cut the meat into reasonable sized chunks and brown well in the melted beef dripping in a thick casserole. Remove the meat and add the sliced onions, reduce the heat and cook gently until they are soft.

Using a pestle and mortar pound the garlic together with the caraway seeds. To me this is one of the most delicious aromas. When they have been well pounded add them to the onions and then add the meat, flour, paprika and the salt and pepper before finally pouring in the stock.

Cook for a few minutes on top of the stove before covering and popping in the oven at 300 f, Gas 2, 150 c, for two-and-a-half to three hours.

Just before serving, stir in the soured cream and serve on a bed of hot buttered noodles.

Delicious on a winter's day.

# Beef Liege

1½ lb lean stewing or braising beef, cut into
   chunks (700 g)
2 ozs lard (50 g)
6 ozs mushrooms (175 g)
6 ozs dried prunes (175 g)
1 garlic clove
1 can of brown ale
bouquet garni
3 onions
½ lb carrots (225 g)
2 teaspoons tomato puree
1 tablespoon plain flour
1 pint of beef stock (570 ml)
salt and black pepper

Choose a casserole dish with a well-fitting lid for
this dish.

In the casserole melt the lard and brown the
meat well. Remove from the pan and set to one
side. Slice the onions, carrot and mushrooms and
fry them gently in the remaining fat adding some
salt and black pepper. Add the crushed garlic.
Remove the vegetables and place with the meat.
Add the flour to the pan and gently cook for one
minute before adding the beer, stock and the rest
of the ingredients. Return the meat and vegetables
to the pan and cook in the oven for one-and-a-
half to two hours at 350 f, Gas 4, 180 c.

# Beef stroganoff

1 lb of lean beef (450 g)
salt and black pepper
1 teaspoon mustard powder
4 ozs butter (110 g)
1 large onion
1 tablespoon plain flour
½ pint of stock (275 ml)
2 tablespoons tomato puree
5 fl ozs soured cream (150 ml)

Cut the beef into thin strips and sprinkle with salt, pepper and the dry mustard. Cut the onion into thin slices and fry gently in 2 ozs (50 g) of the butter. When the onion is soft but not browned stir in the flour and cook for a further minute. Gradually add the stock. Bring to the boil and allow to simmer for one minute or so to cook the flour and to thicken the sauce.

Melt the remaining butter in another thick saucepan and seal the meat on all sides. Stir in the tomato puree and then pour over the onion sauce. Cover and simmer on a very low heat for twenty minutes if using fillet steak, or longer if using a more economical cut as I always do!

Just before you serve this, stir in the soured cream. A treat with hot buttered noodles.

# Meat loaf

1 lb mince, uncooked (450 g)
4 ozs streaky bacon (110 g)
3 slices of bread, soaked in milk and squeezed
   dry
½ teaspoon mixed herbs
1 medium sized onion, chopped
1 large egg
1 garlic clove, chopped
salt and black pepper
1 oz butter (25 g)

Melt the butter in a frying pan or thick saucepan and gently fry the chopped onion and garlic. Cut the bacon into strips and add this to pan and cook for a further two minutes.

In a large bowl, mix the onion and bacon together with all the other ingredients and season well with the salt and pepper.

Press the mixture into a 1 lb loaf tin and cook in the centre of an oven in a bain marie (a roasting pan half-filled with water will do the trick) for one-and-a-half hours at 350 f, Gas 4, 180 c.

Serve either as a sandwich filler or with salad as a lunch dish.

# Flemish carbonade

Serves a houseful of hungry visitors!

3 lb of casserole beef, roughly cut into cubes
(1 kg 350 g)
6 large onions
1 garlic clove, chopped
2 large carrots, sliced
bouquet garni
8 ozs button mushrooms (can be sliced or left
whole) (225 g)
10 very small onions
salt and black pepper
2 ozs butter (50 g)
1 tablespoon flour
1 teaspoon paprika
1 pint of brown ale (570 ml)

In a large, thick casserole gently melt the butter.
Mix the salt, pepper, flour and paprika together
and toss the meat in this. Brown the cubes of
meat on all sides in the butter and then remove
and set to one side. Chop up the large onions and
soften in the remaining butter in the same
casserole before adding the carrots, the chopped
garlic and the mushrooms. Return the meat to
the casserole and pour on the brown ale. Bring to
the boil slowly and allow to boil for one minute,
stirring all the time.

Place the lid on the casserole and put in the

oven at 325 f, Gas 3, 170 c, and cook for two hours.

Serve with baked jacket potatoes.

# Beef casserole with savoury dumplings

1½ lb best stewing steak, cut into fork-sized
   pieces (700 g)
1 large onion, sliced
2 ozs lard (50 g)
8 ozs baby carrots (or sliced-up large ones)
   (225 g)
8 ozs swede or turnip, diced (225 g)
2 ozs plain flour (50 g)
½ pint of brown ale (275 ml)
1 beef stock cube
1 bay leaf
1 teaspoon English mustard powder
salt
black pepper

For the dumplings:
        1 lb mashed potato (450 g)
        4 ozs self-raising flour (110 g)
        1 egg yolk
        1 teaspoon mixed herbs

In a large casserole melt the lard and add the sliced
onion, gently cooking it until it is soft. Add the
baby carrots or the large sliced carrots together
with the diced swede or turnip and cook for a
few minutes longer, stirring all together. Blend in
the flour and, still stirring all the time, allow that
to cook for a minute or two. Add the brown ale

and the beef stock cube together with the mustard, bay leaf and the salt and pepper. Bring to the boil and add the cubed meat to the dish and cover before cooking in the oven at 350 f, Gas 4, 180 c, for about one-and-a-half hours.

In the meantime make the dumplings by mixing the flour and potato together with the mixed herbs. Bind with the egg yolk. You may have to knead these on a floured board. Divide the mixture into twelve and add to the casserole for the final hour of cooking.

A warming dish for a hungry family.

# Veronique's (or Patrick's) chouchouka

2 cups of easy-cook rice
1 lb minced beef (450 g)
1 lb peeled tomatoes (450 g)
2 tablespoons tomato puree
2 garlic cloves
4 medium sized onions, chopped
2 large aubergines
3 courgettes
1 green pepper
1 red pepper
1 teaspoon chili powder
1 teaspoon marjoram
1 teaspoon curry powder
salt and black pepper
½ pint of chicken stock (275 ml)
2 tablespoons oil

In a thick casserole heat the oil and gently fry the mince and the chopped onions until they are brown. Cut all the vegetables into chunks and add to the meat, together with the herbs and spices. Add half the stock and cook on a low heat stirring all the time for no more than ten minutes. Add the rice and the rest of the stock (if you think it necessary) and cook gently until the rice is done. This takes about twenty minutes.

To serve, place in a buttered dish, sprinkle with some grated cheese and breadcrumbs and pop in

a hot oven or under a hot grill for ten minutes.
Serve when the top is nicely browned.

A filling dish for the family.

# Chili beef

1 lb minced beef (450 g)
1 tablespoon oil
1 large onion
1 bay leaf
1 pint of chicken stock (570 ml)
salt and black pepper
½ teaspoon chili powder
1 large tin of red kidney beans
1 large tin of chopped tomatoes
2 tablespoons tomato puree
1 medium sized red pepper
1 tablespoon cornflour

Heat the oil in a thick pan and brown the mince.
Remove from the pan and gently fry the sliced
onion and the red pepper in the oil until they are
soft. Return the meat to the pan and add the rest
of the ingredients, stirring well. Test for
seasoning.

Blend the cornflour with a little water and stir
into the meat mixture and cook gently on the
top of the stove for about forty minutes.

This is really delicious with baked potatoes and
goes well with rice. It also freezes superbly.

# Braised oxtail

2 lb oxtail, chopped (ask your butcher to do
  this for you) (900 g)
2 tablespoons vegetable oil
6 ozs streaky smoked bacon, cut in strips
  (175 g)
6 ozs button mushrooms (175 g)
½ lb carrots (225 g)
2 turnips
1 garlic clove
1 head of celery
½ pint of white wine (275 ml)
1 glass of brandy
10 small onions (pickling size)

Heat the oil in a thick casserole and brown the
chunks of oxtail well. Pour off the excess fat into
a frying pan and pour the brandy on to the meat.
Turn the heat up high and flame the brandy.
Pour on the white wine, adjust the seasoning and
cover and cook in the oven at 350 f, Gas 4, 180 c,
for about two-and-a-half hours.

In a frying pan cook the streaky bacon and stir
in the rest of the sliced vegetables remembering
to leave the onions whole. Place this mixture on
top of the oxtail and cover again and leave in the
oven for another hour until all the flavours
combine and the meat is tender.

Taste and adjust the seasoning before serving
with piping hot, creamed fluffy potatoes.

# Family · Feasting

# PORK

'As a jewel of gold in a swine's snout . . .'
*Proverbs Chapter Eleven*

It is said that you can use every part of the
pig except the curl in its tail. (I am working
on that . . . is it the bend in the sausage?)
To some the pig should never be eaten,
others enjoy it with relish. Consider how
many pork based recipes there are and you
will be surprised.

*RECIPES:*

*Pork envelopes*
*Lemon pork*
*Pork medallions*
*Pork and apple pie*
*Pork chops Abbey Close*
*Sister Sarah's pork plait*
*Pork and bacon loaf*
*Elna's sausage casserole*
*Pork chop casserole*
*Bacon casserole*
*Stuffed bacon chops*

It's very funny the way recipes come into one's hands. Often friends recommend them or you adapt something that takes your fancy. Sometimes when I am shopping in the local supermarket I am pursued by ladies (very delicately, of course) until they decide I am who they think I am and then they pluck up courage to challenge me and comment on this dish or that that they have read in one of my books or seen me prepare on television. I always tread very carefully just in case any recipes of mine have turned out disastrously for others trying them because I forgot to mention a vital ingredient. However, so far such assaults have always led to happy encounters and I have enjoyed meeting and chatting with many delightful ladies!

I always try to encourage them to send me a favourite recipe and to send it as soon as they can. It is a joy to receive their letters and wherever possible to try their recipes.

My mother is now working in a restaurant after her *fifth* retirement! I think she will never really retire and she does love her little part-time job as she is able to learn new recipes and pass on to me some ideas of her own. She is one of those wonderful cooks who always underestimates her ability and has that touch of magic in her fingers so that when the mood takes her (as my father would say), she can produce some wonderful dishes . . . pork is one of her specialities.

The trouble with pork is that some people would say there is not a lot you can do with a chop! I hope some of the following recipes will disprove that.

# Pork envelopes

4 pork chops
4 ozs cooked long grain rice (110 g)
5 ozs cooked sweetcorn (150 g)
5 ozs frozen peas (150 g)
4 spring onions, finely chopped
1 tablespoon Worcestershire sauce
1 wineglass of cider
1 8 oz packet frozen puff pastry (225 g)
1 large egg, well beaten
salt and pepper to taste

Mix the chopped spring onions together with the rice, peas and sweetcorn. Roll out the pastry and divide into four largish squares. Place a chop in each square and sprinkle each one with salt and pepper, a tablespoon of cider, a dash of Worcestershire sauce and place on each a spoonful of the rice and vegetable mixture. With the egg, paint the edges of the pastry and fold in the corners to make a parcel. Seal the edges well.

Pierce the top of the 'envelopes' with a fork and brush all over with the egg. Bake in an oven at 425 f, Gas 7, 220 c, for ten minutes and then turn the oven down to 325 f, Gas 3, 170 c, for a further thirty minutes, coating from time to time with more beaten egg.

A super way to serve pork chops, and even better with a simple apple sauce.

# Lemon pork

2 lb boneless pork, cubed (900 g)
2 tablespoons flour
2 tablespoons vegetable oil
1 tablespoon grated root ginger
2 medium sized onions, sliced
1 large tin of chopped tomatoes
2 tablespoons chopped parsley
4 tablespoons lemon juice
The finely grated rind of a lemon
1 pint of chicken stock (570 ml)
few drops Tabasco sauce
2 tablespoons soured cream

Toss the meat in the flour and season with a little salt and black pepper. Heat the vegetable oil and add the pork and the grated ginger. Cook for a few minutes, turning the meat with a wooden spatula to prevent it sticking. Slice the onions finely and add to the pan together with the tomatoes, parsley, lemon juice and Tabasco sauce. Cook for a few minutes and then add the grated lemon rind. Cook very gently on top of the stove for about an hour, uncovered so that the stock will reduce. Stir regularly, and test the meat for tenderness. The smell is delicious!

Just before serving stir in the soured cream.
This unusual but tasty dish comes from Peru.

# Pork medallions

1½ lbs pork fillet (700 g)
1 oz butter (25 g)
1 tablespoon vegetable oil
1 medium sized onion
1 level tablespoon paprika pepper
2 tablespoons plain flour
4 tablespoons Amontillado sherry
½ pint of stock (275 ml)
4 ozs button mushrooms (110 g)
5 fl ozs of soured cream (150 ml)
salt and black pepper

Melt the butter with the oil in a thick based sauté
or frying pan. Cut the pork fillet into ¾″ (2 cm)
slices or a little thicker or thinner if you prefer,
it really depends on the amount of time that you
have in which to cook them. Brown each
'medallion' on all sides in the oil and butter and
then set aside. Slice the onions and gently cook
for a few minutes in the same pan until they are
transparent and then add the paprika and cook
for a few minutes further. Add the flour and
allow that to cook for a minute being careful to
keep every thing on the move. Slowly add the
stock, a little at a time, and then the sherry until
you have a fairly thickish sauce.

Return the meat to the pan and season with salt
and pepper. Cover and simmer gently for thirty
or forty minutes. Stir frequently. Ten minutes

before the end add the sliced mushrooms and adjust the seasoning.

Serving suggestion: this dish goes very well with creamed potatoes and a simple green salad.

# Pork and apple pie

1 lb pork cubes (boned shoulder is good for this)  (450 g)
1 lb Bramley apples (450 g)
12 ozs potatoes (350 g)
1 large onion
1 chicken stock cube
¼ pint of dry cider (150 ml)
2 ozs plain flour (50 g)
salt and black pepper
3 tablespoons vegetable oil
1 teaspoon dried sage
1 8 ozs packet frozen puff pastry (225 g)

In a thick saucepan heat the oil and brown the cubes of pork and set to one side. Slice the onion and add to the oil and cook gently until softened. Peel and dice the apple and potatoes and add to the onions with a sprinkling of sage. Cook this for about four minutes. Sprinkle in the plain flour and cook for a further minute before gently adding the cider and crumbling in the stock cube. If you find that the sauce is too thick add a little more cider. Season with salt and pepper and return the cubed pork to the pan and heat through for a further couple of minutes before turning the mixture into a pie dish.

Cover with the rolled out puff pastry, sealing the edges well, and bake in the oven at 425 f, Gas 7, 220 c, for twenty minutes and then at 350 f, Gas 4, 180 c, for a further forty minutes.

Quite delicious!

# Pork chops Abbey Close

There is something special about the quality of life in the 'Close' that surrounds each of our cathedrals and large historic abbey churches. It's good to remember that many of them at one time or another were run by worthy monks and friars, so they were in good hands long before the Church of England was even a blush on a merry king's cheek. I said the 'quality' of life is special and indeed some of the clerical antics that go on in them are too . . . the television series of not so long ago was nearer to the truth than many would care to admit!

This dish *Pork chops Abbey Close* hints at but reveals nothing. Well, discretion is the better part of valour. Suffice it to say, sweet and sour experiences both exist! The great thing is though that it all goes to make a harmonious whole . . . read on and you may learn more. . . .

(That's got your appetites whetted!)

4 pork loin chops, trimmed of fat
1 medium sized onion
1 oz butter (25 g)
¼ teaspoon curry paste
1 small can of pineapple chunks
1 wineglass of medium sherry
1 cup of stock or water, plus a stock cube
salt and black pepper

1 heaped teaspoon cornflour mixed with a
   little water

In a shallow, oven-proof dish gently melt the
butter. Add the finely chopped onion and soften
over a low heat. Cook until the onion is opaque.
Add the chops, sherry, stock, salt and pepper
and place in a moderate oven, 375 f, Gas 5, 190 c,
and cook for thirty minutes or so until the chops
are cooked. It may be advisable to turn the chops
once during cooking.

Remove the dish from the oven and place the
chops on a serving dish and keep warm. To the
juices that are left add the curry paste and the
small can of pineapple chunks, together with
their juice, and over a gentle flame thicken the
sauce by adding the cornflour which has been
mixed with a little water. Do make sure that the
cornflour has cooked by letting the sauce bubble
for about a minute.

Pour the sauce over the chops and serve
immediately with some baked jacket potatoes or
plain boiled rice. As with any curry, make sure
there is a plentiful supply of drink and I suggest
the lemon squash found in a later chapter.

# Sister Sarah's pork plait

She wasn't a sister in the strict religious sense, and I do not think her name was Sarah, but what I do remember about this fine old lady who used to join us on the fruit farm during the strawberry-picking season was that she used to bring along cans of fruit to give the multitudes of children who used to throng around her. She had a large broad-rimmed straw hat and wore those incredibly thick stockings. She had a heart of gold, and to me she will always be Sister Sarah. She wore her hair in a plait. . . .

1 8 ozs packet of frozen puff pastry (225 g)
1 lb sausagemeat (450 g)
1 large onion, finely chopped
8 ozs mushrooms (225 g)
1 teaspoon mixed herbs
salt and black pepper
1 oz butter (25 g)

On a well-floured surface, roll out the puff pastry until it makes a large rectangle measuring about 10″ × 14″ (25 cm × 35 cm). Remember when rolling out your pastry never to turn it over. You may turn it round, but not over. Leave the rolled-out pastry to stand in a cool place.

In a thick frying pan melt the butter and add the onion and over a low heat allow it to sweat for a while. Put in a little salt and pepper as well. In the meantime, finely chop the mushrooms and toss in the mixed herbs. You will have to experiment with the family's palate on this one as some like more herbs, and others less. Mix the herb and mushroom mixture together in a bowl with the onion so that they are well blended.

Take the sausage meat and shape it into a rectangle about a third of the width of the pastry and leaving an inch (2.5 cm) at the top and bottom too. Lay the sausagemeat down the centre of the pastry and with the back of a spoon make a channel in the middle of it to accommodate the onion and mushroom mixture. This should run the full length of the sausagemeat.

Now with a sharp knife cut slits of the pastry either side of the sausagemeat starting an inch from the sausagemeat and going to the edge of the pastry, coming down at an angle of about thirty degrees. Do this on both sides. You will need to make about six or eight cuts on each side. Then with a glaze of beaten egg and a little salt, paint the pastry well before folding over the flap of pastry at the top and bottom of the sausagemeat and then crossing over and overlapping the 'fins', just as you would make a plait. When it looks well plaited, carefully place it on a baking tray and coat it well with the beaten egg. Cook in an oven at 450 f, Gas 8, or 230 c for ten minutes before turning the oven down to 300 f, Gas 2, or 150 c and baking it for a further twenty-five minutes.

This is delicious served hot or cold with a crisp green salad.

# Pork and bacon loaf

1 lb minced belly pork (450 g)
½ lb minced back bacon (225 g)
4 ozs fresh breadcrumbs (110 g)
1 onion, finely chopped
1 teaspoon mustard
1 level teaspoon fine herbs
salt and black pepper
1 large egg
¼ pint of cider (150 ml)
1 measure of Calvados (optional)

You may well be able to persuade your butcher to mince the belly pork for you as it is such a fag to remove the skin. Once you have managed to do that, then mix everything together well and allow to stand for about an hour before pressing the mixture into a well greased, two-pound (900 g) loaf tin. Cover the tin with foil and place in a roasting pan half-filled with water in an oven set at 350 f, Gas 4 or 180 c. Cook for two hours.

Place a weight on the top of the baked meat loaf and allow to cool overnight in the tin.

This can be served in handsome slices with a salad.

# Elna's sausage casserole

This little dish always reminds me of New Year celebrations. On one of those mad occasions I scooped up some friends from afar and brought them back for some festivities before returning them well-fed and exercised to their maternal home in Dorset. We managed during their stay to walk up British Camp in the Malverns . . . at least that's where I *think* we went as there was a heavy fog that day.

When we took mother and daughter back home. Elna set about preparing this dish whilst I flitted around the town seeing a few friends and generally trying to spread a little New Year goodwill.

When I returned from my visits this dish was served and certainly does add a new dimension to the good old British banger.

1 lb thin sausages (450 g)
1 medium sized onion
2 large tomatoes, sliced
¼ teaspoon mixed herbs
½ oz butter (50 g)
1 teacup of white wine
1 dessertspoon plain flour
salt and black pepper

In a large, thick casserole dish, melt the butter and gently soften the chopped onion until it is

opaque but not brown. Stir in the flour and add
the wine gradually to make a thickish sauce and
season to taste with salt and black pepper and the
mixed herbs. Cook gently for about a minute
before adding the sausages and tomatoes. Some
people like to brown the sausages a little before
hand, and I must admit it does make them look
a little less anaemic when you serve the dish. Let
the dish simmer on the top of the stove over a
low heat for about twenty minutes or so. Do
make sure that you stir it every few minutes just
to make sure that nothing is sticking at the
bottom of the casserole.

Serve with plain boiled potatoes, mashed or left
whole. A second vegetable which is delicious
with this dish is plain boiled leeks.

It certainly does make sausages more
interesting!

# Pork chop casserole

4 pork chops, trimmed of excess fat
1 medium sized onion, finely chopped
½ pint of medium cider (275 ml)
4 ozs button mushrooms (110 g)
1 large cooking apple, peeled
2 ozs breadcrumbs (50 g)
4 ozs grated cheese (110 g)
6 juniper berries, crushed
1 tablespoon oil
salt and black pepper

Heat the oil in a thick saucepan and add the finely chopped onion and cook gently until soft but not browned. Chop up the apple and the mushrooms and add to the pan and cook for a few minutes longer. Remove from the heat and add a little salt and pepper and pour in the cider. I personally prefer to use a sweet cider but many of my friends prefer the medium variety. Place the chops on the top and then sprinkle on the breadcrumbs and grated cheese which have been mixed with the crushed juniper berries.

Bake in an oven 350 f, Gas 4, 180 c, for one-and-a-half hours.

# Bacon casserole

4 large potatoes
1 lb smoked back or streaky bacon (450 g)
1 lb carrots (450 g)
1 medium onion
salt and black pepper
1 garlic clove finely chopped

Generously butter a large casserole dish. Peel and slice the potatoes, carrots and onion. Using half the quantity of vegetables place a layer of each in the casserole and then sprinkle on the finely chopped garlic. Lay the bacon on top of this and then the rest of the vegetables making sure that you end up with a layer of potatoes on the top.

Dot generously with butter and black pepper and cover. Bake in the oven at 350 f, Gas 4, 180 c for one-and-a-half hours.

# Stuffed bacon chops

5 boneless bacon chops
1 small onion, finely chopped
3 ozs fresh white breadcrumbs (75 g)
1 tablespoon of sultanas
1 egg
2 ozs butter (50 g)
black pepper
6 ozs grated cooking apples (175 g)
The grated rind and juice of a lemon

Use thick bacon chops. These you may have to
ask your butcher to prepare specially for you,
although they are quite common in the North of
England.

Cut from the outside edge into the chop until
you are about half an inch (1 cm) from the inside
edge so as to form a pocket. Make sure that you
cut into the 'eye' of the chop.

Gently fry the finely chopped onion in the
butter until soft but not browned. Mix together
the onion and the grated apple along with the
sultanas, breadcrumbs, black pepper, grated rind
and juice of the lemon. Bind everything together
with the beaten egg.

Place a dessertspoonful of the mixture into the
cavity of each chop. Place the stuffed chops on
a baking tray and bake in the oven for about thirty
minutes at 350 f, Gas 4, 180 c.

As a serving suggestion you can make a
delightful sauce by mixing one tablespoon of

wine vinegar with two tablespoons of honey mixed and a tablespoon of lightly fried, finely chopped onion. Heat this and pour over the chops.

# LAMB

'Your lamb shall be without blemish . . .'
*Exodus Chapter Twelve*

## RECIPES:

*Summerland lamb casserole*
*Moussaka*
*Meatballs of lamb oregano*
*Lamb chops farmhouse style*
*Lamb cutlets in onion sauce*
*Rib of lamb in a spiced sauce*
*Orange glazed lamb*
*Jeremiah's Potter's lamb*
*Lamb stuffed with spinach*
*Lamb chops in apricot sauce*

My father had the distinct advantage of being trained as a butcher when he was a lad, and later in life he became a shepherd. This is marvellous when you take him shopping with you as he knows what he is talking about when it comes to a joint of meat, especially lamb.

In this country we seem to have gone overboard finding the less fat variety and to me this has been a great shame. Some of the finest flavours are found in the fat of the lamb and certainly it does enhance the taste of the meat.

The French eat their lamb almost raw, not a habit that I would like to adopt in spite of my love of the French and their country cooking. There is a splendid and extravagant recipe for *Seven Hour Lamb* that I have not included here as it would have been very costly for a family budget and so I have left it for another occasion.

Minced lamb is superb and certainly makes a little go a long way. It is not as widely available as minced beef, and you may have to convince your butcher that you really *do* want your shoulder of lamb minced. He may prefer you to order it in advance; alternatively you can do it yourself at home. I have used it mixed with ham and pork to make very good patés.

I hope you enjoy these few recipes.

# Summerland lamb casserole

1½ lbs lean lamb, cut in thickish slices (700 g)
2 ozs butter (50 g)
2 tablespoons oil
1 medium sized onion
2 eating apples
2 tablespoons plain flour
1 tablespoon chopped stem ginger
2 tablespoons fresh chopped mint
1 tablespoon brown sugar
½ pint of apple juice (275 ml)
salt and white pepper

Melt the butter and the oil in a thick-based frying
pan or saucepan. Brown the meat well, remove
from the pan and set to one side. Peel and finely
chop the onion and coarsely chop the apples.
Add to the pan and cook for a minute or two.
Stir in the flour and the stem ginger and then
add the mint, sugar and apple juice to make a
fairly thick sauce. Return the meat to the pan
and cover it. Simmer this dish very gently on top
of the stove, stirring frequently, or cook it in the
oven at 375 f, Gas 5, 190 c for approximately an
hour-and-a-half, or until the meat is tender.

Serve with a bed of freshly cooked buttered
noodles.

# Moussaka

1½ lbs minced lamb (700 g)
1 medium sized onion
1 garlic clove
1 large tin of chopped tomatoes
1 teaspoon dried rosemary
1 bay leaf
salt and black pepper
2 large waxy potatoes, peeled and finely sliced
6 ozs grated cheese (175 g)
½ teaspoon grated nutmeg
2 tablespoons vegetable oil

Heat the oil in a thick saucepan.

Finely chop the garlic and onion and gently fry until soft. Add the lamb and cook until it is browned, and then add the tinned tomatoes, herbs, and salt and pepper to taste. Stir well. Bring to the boil and then simmer for about twenty minutes.

In a pan of boiling water very quickly blanch the potatoes and drain them well. Pour the lamb mixture into a casserole dish and cover with the slices of potatoes. Sprinkle with nutmeg before finally topping with the grated cheese.

Place the casserole in an oven preheated to 375 f, Gas 5, 190 c, and bake for forty minutes.

Serve with fresh, crusty bread rolls.

# Meatballs of lamb oregano

2 lbs minced lamb (900 g)
1 large onion, grated
4 ozs cooked rice (110 g)
2 large eggs, beaten
2 tablespoons vegetable oil
1 tablespoon wine vinegar
1 tablespoon finely chopped parsley
6 juniper berries, crushed
½ teaspoon oregano

Sauce:
       1 wineglass of port
       ½ pint of good beef stock (275 ml)
       1 oz flour (25 g)
       1 oz butter (25 g)
       salt and pepper
       1 tablespoon redcurrant jelly

To make the meatballs, gently fry the chopped onion in the vegetable oil and then combine all the other ingredients binding. Roll into balls about the diameter of a five pence piece and flour lightly. Deep-or shallow-fry them in very hot vegetable oil until well browned. Remove the cooked meatballs to a serving dish and keep warm.

For the sauce, melt the butter in a thick saucepan and add the flour, salt, and pepper to form a roux. Cook for one minute then add the stock together with the port and redcurrant jelly. Reduce to a thick pouring consistency and pour over the meatballs.

Serve with a crisp green salad.

# Lamb chops farmhouse style

6 best end of neck lamb chops
3 tablespoons plain flour
2 teaspoons salt
black pepper
2 ozs butter (50 g)
2 tablespoons water
8 ozs mushrooms, finely sliced (225 g)
¼ pint of stock (150 ml)
½ pint of single cream (275 ml)

Mix the flour, salt and pepper together and toss the lamb chops in it. Heat the butter in a large flame-proof casserole and brown the chops well. Remove these from the pan. Add the water, stock and cream to the pan, stirring well and being careful to scrape any little bits of meat or flour away from the base or sides of the pan. Bring to the boil, return the chops to the pan and add the mushrooms.

Place in an oven preheated to 375 f, Gas 5, 190 c and cook for one hour.

Serving suggestion: these are delicious with baked jacket potatoes!

# Lamb cutlets in onion sauce

4 chump cutlets, trimmed of fat

Sauce:

      4 large onions
      1 teaspoon caster sugar
      ½ pint of warmed milk (275 ml)
      2 tablespoons breadcrumbs
      2 ozs finely grated Gruyere cheese
        (50 g)
      salt and black pepper
      2 ozs butter (50 g)
      1 oz flour (25 g)
      ¼ pint of single cream (150 ml)
      water

Sprinkle the cutlets with salt and pepper and bake for about half an hour in a moderate oven, 375 f, Gas 5, 190 c. Leave them in their juices in the baking dish.

For the sauce, peel and slice the onions and boil them for five minutes in a little salted water – just enough to cover them. Then drain them.

Melt half the butter in a thick saucepan and add the onions and sugar and fry for a couple of minutes until soft and buttery. Stir in the flour and cook for one minute. Gradually add the warmed milk, stirring all the time and finally, pour in the cream.

Pour the hot onion sauce over the chops. Mix the breadcrumbs with the Gruyere cheese and sprinkle over the chops and the sauce. Dot with butter, and brown quickly under a hot grill.

Garnish with tomato lilies and serve.

# Rib of lamb in a spiced sauce

1 breast or rib of lamb

Sauce:

> 1 tablespoon clear honey
> 1 tablespoon soy sauce
> 4 tablespoons white wine vinegar
> 1 tablespoon tomato puree
> 1 teaspoon mustard powder
> 1 dessertspoon paprika
> 1 garlic clove, crushed
> salt

For this dish, you can serve the breast of lamb cut into individual ribs, or in a 'crown' shape. If you ask your butcher in advance, he will probably be glad to prepare it to your specification. At home, remove as much fat from the meat as possible, and roast in a hot oven, 400 f, Gas 6, 200 c for an hour if using the joint whole, or for forty-five minutes if cut into ribs.

For the sauce, mix all the ingredients well and coat the cooked meat in it. Pop it back into the oven for ten minutes or brown under the grill. The sauce is delicious mixed with the meat juices.

Serve on a bed of rice.

# Orange glazed lamb

1 3 lb shoulder of lamb, boned (ask your
  butcher to do this) (1 kg 350 g)

Stuffing:

      The grated rind and juice of a large
        orange
      1 oz butter (25 g)
      4 ozs breadcrumbs (110 g)
      1 large onion, finely chopped
      2 ozs sultanas (50 g)
      2 ozs raisins (50 g)
      2 ozs currants (50 g)
      1 teaspoon dried rosemary
      1 tablespoon fresh mint
      salt and black pepper
      1 large egg, beaten

Glaze:

      2 ozs soft brown sugar (50 g)
      juice of 1 orange
      juice of 1 lemon
      2 tablespoons Worcestershire sauce

Sauce:

      4 fl ozs sherry (110 ml)
      ½ pint of beef stock (275 ml)

To prepare the stuffing, put all the dry ingredients
into a large mixing bowl. Add the grated orange
rind and juice, and the chopped onion and bind
everything together well with the beaten egg.

Allow the stuffing mixture to stand for an hour before filling the cavity of the lamb with it. Using fine string, tie into a neat shape or secure with skewers.

Place the joint in a roasting tray.

To make the glaze, place all the ingredients in a thick saucepan and heat over a low flame for a few minutes until hot and well-blended, and then spoon over the meat in the baking dish, taking care to coat the meat on all sides.

Roast the joint in the centre of the oven at 375 f, Gas 5, 190 c, for about two hours, basting frequently.

At the end of the cooking time, remove the joint from the roasting dish and keep hot. Into the pan juices stir the sherry and beef stock and with a wooden spatula, scrape any little bits of meat or glaze away from the base of the dish. Correct the seasoning and boil for a couple of minutes to reduce slightly.

Serve the joint decorated with slices of orange and sprigs of mint, and the sauce separately.

It is good to serve a rich dish like this with something simple, like a side salad and fresh bread.

# Jeremiah's potter's lamb

1 leg of lamb, or a large shoulder
2 garlic cloves, thinly sliced
1 large carrot, sliced
2 stalks of celery, roughly chopped
1 large can of tomatoes
2 large onions, sliced
½ teaspoon turmeric
½ cup of lime or lemon juice
½ teaspoon saffron
(2 ozs butter) (50 g)
(1 tablespoon olive oil)

Choose a large casserole dish with a close fitting lid for this dish.

Make about fifteen slits in the meat with a sharp knife, and insert into each opening a slither of garlic. Place the joint in the casserole and surround with the carrot, onions, celery, can of tomatoes, salt and pepper. Add the turmeric, saffron and the lime or lemon juice. Cover and bake in the oven at 350 f, Gas 4, 180 c, for two-and-a-half to three hours. It may be necessary to add a little water from time to time.

When the meat is well-cooked, remove it from the pan and reduce the juices until you are left with a thick vegetable sauce.

Carve the meat and serve with the vegetables with rice and olives. Delicious!

(This can be adapted for a barbecue party. When the joint is removed from the oven, fix it on long skewers, baste with a mixture of the butter and olive oil, and turn over a charcoal fire.)

# Lamb stuffed with spinach

1 boned leg or shoulder of lamb

Stuffing:

        1 8 ozs packet frozen spinach (225 g)
        1 small onion, chopped
        1 oz butter
        5 fl ozs soured cream (150 ml)
        8 ozs sausagemeat (225 g)
        1 garlic clove, crushed
        ground nutmeg
        salt and black pepper

Ask your butcher (in advance) to bone the joint for you.

To make the stuffing, thaw the packet of spinach. In a frying pan melt the butter and gently fry the chopped onion and the garlic. Then add the nutmeg, spinach and salt and pepper. Remove from the heat and place in a bowl. Mix in the sausagemeat and the soured cream. Cover and allow to stand for a few minutes.

Stuff this mixture into the cavity of the meat and sew or tie up well.

Roast the joint in the oven at 350 f, Gas 4, 180 c, for twenty-five minutes per pound and twenty-five minutes over.

Make a gravy with the juices and serve piping hot.

# Lamb chops in apricot sauce

6 lamb chops
6 ozs dried apricots (175 g)
1 oz butter (25 g)
3 onions, sliced
1 garlic clove
3 tablespoons vinegar
1 oz brown sugar (25 g)
1 tablespoon curry powder
salt and pepper
juice of a lemon

Place the chops in a shallow dish.

Soak the apricots until plump, and puree them in a food processor. Gently fry the onions in the melted butter. Using the food processor again, blend together all the ingredients and pour the mixture over the chops and leave to marinate overnight.

The following day . . . remove the chops and grill them under a hot grill. Gently heat the marinade and pour over the cooked chops.

Super on a cold winter's day.

# DESSERTS

'Out of the strong came forth sweetness . . .'
*Judges Chapter Fourteen*

Alas cream, as such, is mentioned nowhere in
the Bible but we can be sure that the Eastern
palate had many sweet desires. Here are a
selection of dishes that may lead you into
temptation.

### RECIPES:

*Pamplemousse mousse*
*The Heathen's Hope*
*The Vicar's Vow*
*Free Church pudding*
*Heavenly afters*
*The Dean's cream*
*Peach and cider syllabub*
*Friar William's pear delight*
*Grapefruit and elderflower water ice*
*Lemon custard tart*
*Christmas puddings*

Children, both old and young, never need much encouragement when it comes to eating puddings. At the vicarage we have a rule that the youngest person always gets served first with dessert.

I must admit we have let our hair down a little in naming some of these recipes, but that is meant to add to the fun. I don't know why so many of them have ended up with names to do with clerics – it hardly seems complimentary to the puddings! *Inspired* is the word I would use for some of these dishes and they really are all very simple.

The French always serve the cheese before the pudding, and, if you think about this, it really does make a good deal of sense. We once made the mistake of doing things the 'English' way in a very exclusive French restaurant and I saw the head waiter almost in tears . . . we never made the same mistake again.

However, when you are at home, you do as you please!

# Pamplemousse mousse

(No, there is no mistake – a pamplemousse is a grapefruit and a mousse is a mousse!!)

1 pint of fresh grapefruit juice (570 ml)
The juice of a lemon
1 oz gelatine (25 g)
3 ozs icing sugar (75 g)
4 egg whites
The grated rind of one grapefruit
black grapes to decorate

Sprinkle the gelatine on a little warm water and leave it to dissolve. Then gently stir this into the grapefruit juice, and add the lemon juice and icing sugar. Mix thoroughly and leave in a refrigerator for a few hours.

When the grapefruit mixture begins to set, whip the egg whites until they are stiff and carefully fold these into the grapefruit mixture. Spoon into individual glasses or into a serving dish and chill well. Decorate with a few black grapes and the grated grapefruit rind.

Turn the page to see what to do with the egg yolks . . . waste not, want not!

# The Heathen's Hope

The proportions of this may seem extravagant, but it is very rich and will go a long way. Hence, it is an ideal party pudding.

1 lb plain chocolate (450 g)
½ lb butter (225 g)
3 egg yolks
1 lb broken ginger biscuits (450 g)
4 ozs chopped almonds (110 g)
4 ozs sultanas (110 g)
4 ozs maraschino cherries (110 g)
4 ozs candied peel (110 g)
a generous measure of orange liqueur
¼ pint of double cream (150 ml)

Break the chocolate into squares and place in a dish over a pan of hot water and allow to melt. Cut up the butter and add this to the hot, melted chocolate and blend together. In a large bowl place the broken biscuits, nuts, fruit, and peel and sprinkle with the liqueur.

Beat the egg yolks into the chocolate and butter mixture and fold into the biscuits, etc. Press into a buttered mould (a large basin or a loaf tin will do) and chill well in the refrigerator. Stand the mould in hot water for a few seconds and turn out the pudding on to a serving dish.

Whip the double cream until thick and pipe over as decoration.

This dish is devilishly good but you will only want a little of it.

# The Vicar's Vow

6 fl ozs of lemon juice (175 ml)
the finely grated rind of three lemons
½ pint of double cream (275 ml)
8 ozs caster sugar (225 g)
¼ pint of water or dry white wine (150 ml)
½ oz gelatine (10 g)

Sauce:

> the grated rind and juice of a large
> orange
> ¼ pint of water (150 ml)
> 2 ozs caster sugar (50 g)
> 1 level teaspoon cornflour
> pinch of salt
> ½ oz butter (10 g)

Blend together the lemon juice, lemon rind, caster
sugar and double cream until the mixture begins
to thicken. Gently heat the gelatine over a low
flame in the water or wine, and when it is
completely dissolved, whisk it into the cream
mixture. Pour into a litre-sized mould and chill
in a refrigerator. Dip the mould in hot water for
a few seconds and turn out the cream on to a
serving dish.

For the sauce, begin by blending together the
cornflour and the water; stir in the rest of the
ingredients except the orange rind and heat over
a low flame until the sauce begins to thicken.

Just before you are ready to serve, sprinkle in the orange rind.

Serve the hot sauce with the chilled lemon cream. It's divine!!

# Free Church pudding

I think it's almost a sin that we have virtually lost sight of the traditional steamed pudding. What could be more satisfying, and indeed nutritious, than a good old-fashioned steamed pudding that will comfort and sustain you during a long winter's evening? I wouldn't recommend anything like jogging after indulging in a portion, but it certainly would help before bell-ringing practice despite its Free Church title!

4 ozs breadcrumbs (110 g)
4 ozs caster sugar (110 g)
4 ozs grated suet (110 g)
1 teaspoon ground ginger
2 eggs
4 ozs plain flour (110 g)
4 ozs currants (110 g)
2 ozs candied peel (50 g)
2 tablespoons golden syrup
½ teaspoon bicarbonate of soda or baking
   powder
2½ fl ozs of milk (65 ml)

Mix together in a bowl the breadcrumbs, sugar, flour and ginger. Rub the suet into the flour and add the dried fruit, peel and bicarbonate of soda or baking powder. Stand the tin of syrup in a little bowl of hot water before putting two tablespoons of it into a separate basin with the milk and eggs. Mix these together and then blend with the dry ingredients.

Press firmly into a buttered pudding basin and cover with foil.

Steam for two hours and serve with hot custard . . . filling and warming in cold weather.

# Heavenly afters

½ pint of double cream (275 ml)
4 ozs broken meringue pieces (110 g)
2 ozs caster sugar (50 g)
2 tablespoons orange liqueur

Beat the cream until it is stiff and then gently fold in the rest of the ingredients.

Freeze for at least two hours.

Remove from the freezer about fifteen minutes before serving.

Serving suggestion: melt half a pound (225 g) of plain chocolate in a bowl over hot water and pour over as a tempting sauce!

# The Dean's cream

It is daunting for any young lass to marry into a clergy family . . . especially when the prospective father-in-law turns out to be the Dean of the diocesan cathedral! However, one young lady, whose courage I admire enormously, willingly took on the task and has managed to cope with the eccentricities of clerical life with great aplomb. This dish is dedicated to her and her father-in-law . . . I think you will agree with me that she has found out his weakness!!

8 trifle sponges
2 ozs strawberry jam (50 g)
2 ozs orange marmalade (50 g)
2 ozs ratafia biscuits (50 g)
5 fl ozs sweet sherry (150 ml)
the juice and grated rind of a lemon
2 ozs caster sugar (50 g)
3 tablespoons white wine
3 tablespoons brandy
½ pint of double cream (275 ml)
To decorate: cherries, toasted almonds and
    angelica

Spread half the sponge cakes with jam, and half with marmalade, and arrange them in layers in a deep glass dish. Scatter over the ratafia biscuits and sprinkle with the sherry. Whip the cream until thick and fold in the white wine, brandy, lemon juice and rind, sugar. Pour this mixture

over the sponge base with the cream mixture.
Cover and leave to chill in the refrigerator
overnight.

Decorate before serving.

I am told this will satisfy six to eight *normal*
appetites!

# Peach and cider syllabub

½ pint of double cream (275 ml)
2 ozs caster sugar (50 g)
¼ pint of medium dry cider (150 ml)
¼ oz gelatine (5 g)
1 small tin of peaches

Dissolve the gelatine in a very little warm water.
Drain the peaches and cut into small pieces. In
a mixing bowl, place the cream, sugar, cider and
gelatine and beat until well stiffened. Finally stir
in the peaches and spoon into tall serving glasses.
Chill well.

# Friar William's pear delight

If my car had not decided to give up the ghost in the South of France, I may never have discovered the delights of really good pears and the delicious liqueur that the French make from them. On second thoughts, though, I guess that it would only have been a matter of time!

However, this deliciously tangy sweet makes good use of over-ripe pears which can sometimes be difficult to cope with.

It came to me as a pleasant surprise from a hostess who kindly entertained me at one of the 'Cook-Ins' I do throughout the country.

6 ripe William pears
½ pint of double cream (275 ml)
the grated rind and juice of a large orange
1 tablespoon pear liqueur

Peel and halve the pears; scoop out the cores, and place them in a serving dish.

Whip the cream until it is thick and fold in the pear liqueur and the orange rind.

Squeeze the juice of the orange over the pear halves and then cover with the cream mixture.

Place in a refrigerator and chill overnight.

# Grapefruit and elderflower waterice

1 pint of water (570 ml)
10 ozs caster sugar (275 g)
the juice of a lemon
2 egg whites, stiffly beaten
the finely pared rind and juice of two
   grapefruit
8 heads of elderflower

Put the sugar and the water into a large, thick
saucepan. Add the rind of the grapefruit and set
over a low flame, stirring until the sugar is
dissolved. Turn up the heat, bring it to the boil
and bubble rapidly for five minutes. Remove from
the heat.

Remove the elderflowers from their stalks (with
the aid of a fork) and place them in a muslin bag.
Steep them in the hot liquid for ten minutes or
so, then remove. Add the grapefruit and lemon
juices. Leave to stand until completely cold.

Strain the syrup through a nylon sieve on to
the beaten egg whites. Carefully fold together.
Put in the freezer and then bring out after forty
minutes or so and beat well until white and
creamy. Refreeze until firm.

# Lemon custard tart

1 pint of milk (570 ml)
4 egg yolks
3 ozs caster sugar (75 g)
the juice and grated rind of a lemon
A little grated nutmeg

Pastry:

> 6 ozs self-raising flour (175 g)
> 3 ozs butter (75 g)
> 2 ozs caster sugar (50 g)
> 1 egg
> 1 tablespoon milk

To make the pastry, mix together the flour and the sugar. Rub in the butter until the mixture resembles breadcrumbs and bind with the egg. If necessary, use the milk to add a little more moisture.

Roll out the pastry and use it to line an eight (20 cm) or ten-inch (25.5 cm) flan dish.

For the filling, beat together the egg yolks and the sugar and add the juice and rind of the lemon. Finally, add the milk. (Depending on the size and depth of your flan case, you may need slightly less than a pint (570 ml).)

Sprinkle on some grated nutmeg and bake in the oven at 375 f, Gas 5, 190 c, for about thirty minutes, or until the custard filling is set.

Allow to chill.

Ideal on hot summer days.

# Christmas puddings

These can be made well in advance of Christmas: the flavour improves with keeping!

1 lb large raisins (450 g)
2 ozs mixed peel (50 g)
2 ozs chopped blanched almonds (50 g)
½ lb currants (225 g)
½ lb sultanas (225 g)
¼ lb self-raising flour (110 g)
½ level teaspoon ground nutmeg
½ level teaspoon mixed spice
½ level teaspoon ground cinnamon
1 teaspoon salt
2 ozs ground almonds (50 g)
1 lb shredded suet (450 g)
½ lb fresh white breadcrumbs (225 g)
¼ lb soft dark brown sugar (110 g)
6 large eggs
4 tablespoons of brandy
8 fl ozs of stout (225 ml)
2 ozs slightly salted butter (50 g)

Mix together the raisins, peel, chopped almonds, currants, sultanas, self-raising flour, nutmeg, mixed spice, cinnamon, salt, ground almonds, shredded suet, fresh breadcrumbs, and soft brown sugar. The only real way to mix this is by rolling up your sleeves and using your hands! Leave the mixture to stand for an hour.

Mix together well the eggs, stout and brandy and add this to the dry ingredients. Stir everything until the mixture has a dropping consistency, plopping heavily off the wooden spoon. The aroma at this point will be delicious.

Butter well two 2½ pint (1 litre 425 ml) pudding basins and fill them with the mixture to within an inch of the top. Cover these with a foil lid with a pleat in it to allow the puddings to expand. Secure with string, and steam for at least six hours.

Allow to cool, and store in a cool dry place.

Steam for a further four hours on Christmas day.

# Family · Feasting
# CHEESE

'Carry these cheeses to the Captain . . .'
*1 Samuel Chapter Eighteen*

A personal reflection upon some great
cheeses.

# Cheeses

I doubt very much if the Captain who received the cheese that David took to him would make much of the cheeses that we mass produce in Britain today. At times, I too despair at the way our cheeses are made, presented and handled in today's vast consumer markets. There have been some glimmers of light in recent years, with courageous small-holders fighting back and making gallant efforts to produce the 'real thing' once again. Unfortunately however, with the demise of the traditional art of cheese-making, went many of the skills associated with it, and much of the handed-down knowledge and experience which could judge when a cheese was in perfect condition for selling.

Some people who have gone into cheese-making today, have begun their craft from an idealistic outlook, satisfying their own desire to 'get back to nature', and it has often resulted in the blind leading the blind. However, I don't mean to discourage them, after all they are spearheading the campaign for real cheese.

When I lived in the North of England, I delighted in the fact that at many of the small rural agricultural shows there were small traders setting up stalls and selling their home-made cheeses. One of the most successful was a sheep's milk cheese from just north of the border in Annan. Again, just recently, I heard on the radio of a farmer in Northern Ireland who was setting about to use his ewes' milk for cheese production. Cheese made from this milk has a deliciously strong flavour and a good 'bite'. I feel it is an acquired taste.

I wish all cheese-makers well, especially the lady whom I interviewed in Cumbria, who has been trying to recreate genuine farmhouse Cheddar. She has won many fights against the agricultural authorities and I hope that her efforts continue. I didn't ask her where she got her milk from . . . I didn't think the EEC would like her answer!

My many trips to France and my encounters with a tremendous number of unofficial local cheeses, only goes to prove that the long arm of European law in Brussels is thankfully having little effect on the skill and dignity of the local agricultural worker in France who delights in his local cheese which so often compliments the local wine. Unlike wine, these cheeses will never travel, and I thank goodness for that as otherwise their popularity would ruin them, and the genuine article would be buried under attempts at mass production. Like the great masters, reproductions are only pale copies of the real thing. Let them slip by unnoticed; it's best for all concerned.

It would be wrong of me to start my list of cheeses with a continental variety when so many fine cheeses reside and have their origin firmly in this country; so let's begin at the heart of things.

### English Cheddar

The traditional home of the English Cheddar is Somerset and is now made largely in factories and more rarely on the traditional farm. The traditional form of Cheddar is a tall cylinder, but imported and other mass-produced Cheddars are made in oblong blocks, for the obvious reason that it

141

enables them to be stored and transported more easily. The traditional farmhouse Cheddar is fourteen to sixteen inches in diameter and as many inches tall, weighing in at between sixty-six and seventy-seven pounds, and cloth-wrapped.

A good Cheddar takes about six months to mature in cool dry cellars and it is when it leaves the security of its home that many a good Cheddar deteriorates horribly. When the cheese is wrapped in plastics and stored in airless refrigerator units, then untold damage is done to the flavour and texture. Traditionally it is naturally cured in the cellar. The texture of the rind should be smooth and slightly waxy, with a firm oily feel to it and a slight aroma. Although the taste should be pronounced, it should not be very spicy as many imported strong cheddars seem to be.

Cheddar is traditionally served at the end of meals, at breakfasts (would you believe) as well as for snacks and on picnics. It's also good with some sweet dishes. Try a piece of tasty farmhouse cheddar with apple pie, its an excellent combination.

If you are taking it with wine, choose a rounded and robust red wine to complement the cheese. Personally, I always feel happier eating Cheddar with a barley wine or strong export beer.

Cheddar has family links with the cheeses of Cheshire, Leicester and Gloucester differing in origin, shape, colour and flavour. It is one of our most versatile and useful cheeses, and is often abused by the cook!!

# The Great Cheshire Cheese

There is every reason for the Cheshire Cheese to have a grin on its face as proverbial as the cat of the same name, as unlike the Cheddar (which, incidentally, is also made in France as well as the countries of the Commonwealth), it is uniquely and authentically English. It carries in its name its traditional county home, but Cheshire is also copied in Shropshire and other nearby counties. A good Cheshire takes up to two years to mature and should make the tip of your tongue tingle when you eat it.

Once again, this cheese is now made almost entirely in factories which is really a great shame for it has a magnificent history. The family skills that went into making this fine cheese have probably been lost for ever.

Cheshire is an all-year-round cheese and thrives no better in any particular season. Like the traditional Cheddar, it is cloth-wrapped and of a similar size, although heavier weighing from seventy-seven to eighty-eight lbs.

It is slightly oily, but firm with a slight smell and sweet bouquet. It is the traditional cheese to use for Welsh Rarebit.

There is a white, faster-curing variety but I am not a fan of that and normally leave it well alone. Seek out the *real* Cheshire and grin like the Cheshire Cat yourself, in satisfaction.

# Stilton

What can be said about this cheese? I have discovered that my three selected English cheeses are the only cheeses mentioned in my French dictionary of cheeses – commendation indeed.

Leicestershire is the home of the Stilton and the place of manufacture provides the name. A real farmhouse Stilton takes a careful nine months to mature, but so called progress has reduced this in commercial production to one third of that time. I can't think that that is a good thing. If a cheese isn't ready for eating, I can't help feeling it's better to wait for the real thing. Prince Charles recently opened a new Stilton 'factory' in Leicestershire. I can only lament such an enterprise. Look at the abused Stilton we so often obtain in our shops . . . making it should be a work of art rather than a conveyor-belt job.

Once again it was traditionally made in the shape of a cylinder, about six inches in diameter and ten inches high, unwrapped, and was pierced from time to time to allow air in to stimulate the bacteria to do their work of creating the mould, distinctive aroma and spicy flavour.

There are stories of Stilton being soaked in Port, but I much prefer to drink my port with Stilton and dry biscuits (preferably high baked water biscuits), . . . but for a change, if you do not feel a leaning to Port, Madeira complements it well.

### French cheese

Of the wealth of French cheeses, I will strictly limit myself to three and begin with perhaps the most common . . . the Brie. But when is a Brie not a Brie? – There are many wolves in sheep's clothing, and the choice or determination of the original is made all the more difficult by supermarkets cutting up and pre-packing the cheese and its identifying label into portions. Let me try to sort out the riddle.

If you have a good delicatessen that can show you the whole cheese, its label should read 'Brie' or 'Department of Seine et Marne'. If these words appear, there is then no problem, you have the real thing. There are other cheaper varieties, but this is the real McCoy.

Farmhouse Bries are a rare and exceptional treat even in France. Although 'farmhouse Bries' seem to be appearing in our supermarkets just now, I really would have to question their fine-sounding definition, as they are nothing like the farmhouse Bries I have tasted in Seine et Marne itself. The genuine ones are rare and quite expensive.

The Brie is a delicious cheese and my belief is that it should be eaten in long slithers or fingers, with white grapes and, if you have to have a biscuit, a Bath Oliver. To my palate this is one of the most sublime tastes. A good fresh Brie should have no scent of ammonia about it, and a perfectly edible milky-white outer layer. I could go on but I must not . . . just be careful and try to buy your Brie from the delicatessen. It almost makes me weep when I see it wrapped and suffocated in foil on supermarket shelves.

## Camembert

My many trips to Normandy, France's exquisite dairy region has opened the door to some superb enjoyment of this delicious cheese. Contrary to popular belief, it is not the smelly, runny concoction so often found in this country, but a mild, deliciously tasty cheese that goes down well with crispy French Bread. No butter is required . . . who needs butter on their bread with cheeses as delicious as those you can buy in France? The very best is the Camembert Fermier, made often from untreated grass and non-pasteurised milk. To enjoy it at its best, I think it should be tackled when it is still slightly young, but that is a personal preference and not every Frenchman would go along with me.

It is a surprisingly quick-maturing cheese: between four and five weeks in cool, dry cellars is all it needs, but having experienced some blistering Normandy summers I do wonder if they manage to keep their cellars cool for that length of time!

Camembert is, surprisingly enough, a relatively young cheese as cheeses in France go. It is said that in 1791, Marie Harel, a farm woman of the village of Camembert, invented this cheese and gave the recipe to her daughter, who married Victor Paynel. For some reason I have yet to unearth, a statue was erected to her by four hundred cheesemakers from Van Wert in Ohio U.S.A., in the French town of Mimoutiers at a cost of 2,800 dollars. What brought Camembert to the markets of the world was the invention of the round cylindrical box by Monsieur Ridel of Marseilles. Previously it was wrapped in straw which made it impossible to carry it further than Paris.

A delightful cheese then, and one which I have found to be popular with the hordes of English children I have taken to France in the past, provided of course they have had plenty of crusty French bread to go with it.

If you do happen to have some Camembert that gets over-ripe, then mash it in with some potatoes and roll out some croquettes. Coat them in breadcrumbs and fry them in oil. They taste delicious.

A good Camembert cheese should be regular in

shape. A small cylindrical disc, 4½ inches across and 1¼ inches thick, weighing about nine ounces. It should have a downy white surface and feel supple, not soft, with a tangy fragrance, and fruity flavour.

## Ami de Chambertin
Limiting myself to six cheeses has been a most frustrating and impossible exercise. Let me share a little of my frustration with you. A couple of years ago we were making our annual Pilgrimage to the South of France and stayed overnight at the delightful town of Tournos, just over half way down on the left, as my companion said when he was describing it to some of our friends. This is a Romanesque town in the Burgundian style that I love so much. There is a fine Cathedral and an impressive array of little streets huddled beside the river Soane.

We stayed at a little hotel in complete peace . . . although we were a little apprehensive at first as we were led away from the main hotel to a little, ramshackle side-street. But we soon found ourselves in the most delightful little cottage that had been converted into an annexe by the hotel. It was peaceful after the incessant drone of the motorway/autoroute traffic and here we rested, looking on to a postage stamp-sized garden before we dined.

The meal was simple and honest, and served by a girl who had come from Bolton a couple of years earlier. She had fallen in love with the place and decided to stay.

We had a bottle of Chambertin, and she suggested a cheese . . . 'Ami de Chambertin'. It was a taste of heaven. I have never found it anywhere else and I long to go back to try it again. Perhaps I shall. . . .

# Family · Feasting

# CAKES

'Take fine flour and bake twelve cakes . . .'
*Leviticus Chapter Twenty-Four*

And we shall do just that, but will probably
end up with more than twelve!

### RECIPES:

*Eve's tempting cake*
*Welsh love cake*
*Simnel cake*
*Angel cake*
*Bible cake*
*Apricot cake*
*Margaret Robinson's very own Black Forest
gateau*
*Churchwarden's cake*
*Devil's food cake*
*Hot cross buns*

I lament the passing of the tradition of having tea at four. What a far more civilised place this world would be if we did manage to stop properly for half an hour in the afternoon and partake of one of the niceties of life.

Imagine factories all over the country with Palm Court Tea Rooms. I am sure there would be an increase in production and it would make the noisy surroundings of industry more bearable . . . but the ever-hungry giant of the national economy would never allow it.

How sad it is too that the art of cake-making is also taking a bit of a back seat, especially as it is now so easy to buy the commercial, ready-baked varieties. In this section we hope to redress the balance a little, and encourage people to have a go for themselves once again.

Some of the cakes have a religious significance, like the Simnel cake where the eleven balls of marzipan represent the eleven disciples who were left after Judas Iscariot had left their company. There is a story about the Scripture cake too . . . but there are many stories about that. I believe it simply was an invention to amuse the children while mother was in the kitchen: they had the task of looking up the ingredients from the references in the Bible.

I do hope you will try some of these recipes.

# Eve's tempting cake(!!!)

12 ozs self-raising flour (350 g)
8 ozs caster sugar (225 g)
5 ozs butter (150 g)
2 egg yolks, beaten
pinch of salt

Apple filling:
> 1 lb Bramley apples (450 g)
> the juice of a lemon
> ¼ teaspoon grated nutmeg
> 2 ozs raisins (50 g)

Topping:
> 3 ozs chopped hazelnuts (75 g)
> 3 tablespoons apricot jam
> 3 ozs icing sugar (75 g)
> 2 tablespoons cherry brandy

Mix the flour and sugar and salt, rub in the butter and bind together into a dough with the egg yolks. Knead well and then leave to cool for a few minutes in the refrigerator.

Gently stew the apples together with the lemon juice, nutmeg and raisins.

Roll out half the dough and line a ten inch flan case. Bake blind in the oven for fifteen minutes at 400 f, Gas 6, 200 c.

Allow the apple mixture to cool and spread this

151

on top of the pastry. Use the rest of the pastry to roll out a lid and cover the apple. Bake for a further half-hour, keeping the oven at the same temperature.

Warm the jam and spread this over the cooked cake. Sprinkle over half the nuts and then blend the icing sugar with the cherry brandy and spread it over the cake. Sprinkle the rest of the nuts on the top.

Scrumptious if eaten warm.

# Welsh love cake

Pastry:

> 8 ozs plain flour (225 g)
> 4 ozs butter (110 g)
> 1 large egg
> 2 ozs caster sugar (50 g)
> 1 drop vanilla essence
> a little water

Apple puree:

> 1 lb apples (450 g)
> 4 ozs sugar (110 g)
> ¼ teaspoon cinnamon
> 1 oz butter (25 g)

Filling:

> 4 ozs caster sugar (110 g)
> 6 ozs icing sugar (175 g)
> 4 ozs self-raising flour, sifted (110 g)
> the grated rind and juice of a lemon
> 4 ozs butter (110 g)
> 2 large eggs

Peel and slice the apples, and in a thick saucepan gently cook them together with the butter, caster sugar, cinnamon and the hint of a drop of water. Allow to cool and puree.

Make the pastry in the usual way, and line a ten inch (25.5 cm) flan dish with it. (I usually do this in a food processor, throwing in all the ingredients and just turning the switch until it forms a ball!!)

Spread the puree on top of the pastry.

For the filling, cream together the butter, caster sugar and grated rind of the lemon. Whisk the eggs well and fold these into the mixture along with the sifted flour. Spread this mixture on top of the apple.

Bake in the oven at 375 f, Gas 5, 190 c for twenty-five minutes.

Mix the lemon juice and icing sugar to make a thin icing to pour over the cake while it is still warm.

Enough to make any Welshman fall in love.

# Simnel cake

A traditional cake to serve on Mothering Sunday or at Easter.

8 ozs plain flour (225 g)
pinch of salt
½ teaspoon grated nutmeg
½ teaspoon cinnamon
12 ozs currants (350 g)
6 ozs sultanas (175 g)
3 ozs mixed peel (75 g)
6 ozs butter (175 g)
6 ozs caster sugar (175 g)
3 eggs
milk to mix

Almond Paste:
> 12 ozs caster sugar (350 g)
> 8 ozs ground almonds (225 g)
> 1 egg, beaten
> lemon juice

Set the oven at 325 f, Gas 3, 170 c.

Grease an eight-inch (20 cm) cake tin and line with greaseproof paper.

Make the almond paste by simply mixing the ingredients into a pliable paste. Halve the almond paste and roll one half into a round the diameter of the cake tin.

To make the cake, cream together the sugar and butter and beat in the eggs. Add the flour, fruit and the rest of the ingredients. Mix to a consistency that will drop off the spoon easily. Put half the mixture in the cake tin. Cover this with the rolled out almond paste and then put in the rest of the cake mixture and bake in the oven for three hours.

When the cake is cool, cover with more almond paste making sure you reserve enough to make the balls for the top of the cake: eleven for Easter or twelve for Mothering Sunday.

Brush the marzipan with a little beaten egg and brown under the grill.

# Angel cake

11 egg whites
¼ lb plain flour (110 g)
10 ozs caster sugar (275 g)
1 teaspoon cream of tartar
1 teaspoon vanilla essence
pinch of salt

Topping:
8 ozs icing sugar (225 g)
1 teaspoon vanilla essence
the juice of a lemon
1 egg yolk

Whip the egg whites long and well until they are
stiff enough to support the weight of two eggs
in their shells. Sift the flour four or five times as
well. Finally sift the flour and sugar together a
couple of times with the pinch of salt.

Fold the sugar and flour into the egg whites,
and add the vanilla essence. Pour the mixture
into an ungreased ring tin and bake in an oven at
350 f, Gas 4, 180 c for forty-five minutes. Test
with a skewer before removing from the oven: if
the skewer comes out of the cake dry, it is done.

Make the icing by blending the other
ingredients and coat the cake.

This cake is very moreish and delightfully light.
It is quite something else – but then it is
American!

# Bible cake

Bible cake, or Scripture cake as it is sometimes known, seems to have sprung into existence as a form of Victorian piety and it has gone on and on. The earliest records of it I have managed to find are in Peterborough, where it is found in a recipe book that was produced to raise money for a local hospital, at the beginning of the Victorian period.

It is fun to make because it can involve the whole family – children find it interesting to look up the references.

This version of the recipe is particularly tasty.

If you don't want to look up the Bible references, there is a list of the ingredients at the back of the book – but that is cheating!

# Bible cake

½ lb Judges 5, verse 25 (225 g)
½ lb Jeremiah 6, verse 20 (225 g)
1 tablespoon 1 Samuel 14, verse 25
3 Jeremiah 17, verse 11
½ lb 1 Samuel 30, verse 12 (225 g)
½ lb Nahum 3, verse 12 (225 g)
2 ozs Numbers 17, verse 8 (50 g)
1 lb 1 Kings 4, verse 22 (450 g)
Season with 2 Chronicles 9, verse 9
pinch of Leviticus 2, verse 13
1 teaspoon Amos 4, verse 5
1 tablespoon Judges 4, verse 19

Mix as for a fruit cake and place in an 8″ (20 cm)
cake tin and bake for one-and-a-half hours at
325 f, Gas 3, or 170 c.

# Apricot cake

7 ozs self-raising flour (200 g)
4 ozs cherries (110 g)
1 large tin of apricots
2 large eggs
2 tablespoons milk
4 ozs sultanas (110 g)
4 ozs raisins (110 g)
4 ozs currants (110 g)
5 ozs butter (150 g)
4½ ozs caster sugar (420 g)

Grease a 2 lb (900 g) loaf tin with butter.

Set the oven at 325 f, 170 c, Gas 3.

Cream together the butter and the sugar. Beat in the eggs and with the last egg add one tablespoonful of flour. Fold in the rest of the flour, milk, strained apricots and the fruit except for the cherries. Place the mixture in the tin and arrange the cherries in a row along the top.

Bake in the centre of the oven for two hours.

# Margaret Robinson's very own Black Forest gateau

Sponge mixture:

> 4 ozs caster sugar (110 g)
> 4 ozs butter (110 g)
> 4 ozs self-raising flour (110 g)
> 2 large eggs, beaten
> 1 teaspoon baking powder
> 2 heaped dessertspoons cocoa
>   powder
> 1 tablespoon hot water

Beat the sugar and butter well together until smooth and creamy. Add the eggs gradually and beat thoroughly for a few minutes. Sieve the flour with the baking powder and cocoa into the mixture and beat until smooth before adding the hot water and beating again. Pour the mixture into two prepared seven-inch (18 cm) sandwich tins and bake at 400 f, Gas 6, 200 c for twenty minutes. When cool, split each sponge into two.

Filling:

> 1 can of blackcurrant pie filling.
> 12 ozs double cream (350 g)
> 1 oz caster sugar (25 g)
> a drop of vanilla essence.

Beat the cream, sugar and essence together until

thick. Assemble the gateau, putting a layer of blackcurrant and the cream mixture between each sponge half.

Icing:

> 1 teaspoon melted butter
> 1 tablespoon hot water
> 4 ozs icing sugar (110 g)
> 1 dessertspoon cocoa powder

Beat the ingredients thoroughly together. When they are smoothly blended and the icing looks shiny, pour it over the cake and then sprinkle it with grated dark chocolate.

# Churchwarden's cake

8 ozs plain chocolate (225 g)
8 ozs butter (225 g)
8 ozs wholewheat biscuits (digestives),
  broken into small pieces (225 g)
2 eggs
2 dessertspoons caster sugar
1 oz chopped walnuts (25 g)

Melt the chocolate in a dish over hot water. In a separate pan, melt the butter and remove from the heat. Beat in the eggs and sugar and then the melted chocolate. Do make sure that you beat well all the time.

Fold in the broken biscuits and chopped walnuts.

Pour the mixture into a small, square cake tin and allow to set in a cool place.

Cut in fingers to serve.

# Devil's food cake

8 ozs self-raising flour (225 g)
12 ozs caster sugar (350 g)
6 ozs butter (175 g)
3 eggs
¼ pint of milk (150 ml)
pinch salt
1 teaspoon baking powder
6 tablespoons cocoa

Preheat the oven to 350 f, Gas 4, 180 c.

To make the cake, blend together well the sugar and butter until they are really light and creamy. Separate the eggs and beat the yolks into the milk. Gradually add this to the butter and sugar mixture, beating all the time. Sift together the flour, cocoa and salt, and mix this in. Whisk the egg whites until they stand up in peaks and then fold these into the cake mixture. Lightly grease an eight-inch (20 cm), deep cake tin and pour in the mixture. Bake the cake for about one-and-a-half hours. When cool, cut into three equally-sized layers.

For the filling:
> 4 ozs butter (110 g)
> 4 ozs dark chocolate (110 g)
> 4 ozs soft dark brown sugar (110 g)
> 1 small glass of brandy
> ½ pint of double cream, whipped until thick (275 ml)

In a bowl over some hot water, melt together the butter and chocolate and blend in the brown sugar. Transfer to a thick-bottomed pan and heat thoroughly. Cool a little and fold in the brandy and whipped double cream.

This should be sufficient to put between each layer and to cover the cake entirely. Leave the icing very rough-looking and all will be well, it will look tremendously tempting, and taste as good as it looks!

# Hot cross buns

1 lb wholewheat flour (450 g)
¾ oz yeast (15 g)
2 ozs butter (50 g)
3 ozs chopped peel (75 g)
3 ozs currants (75 g)
3 ozs raisins (75 g)
1 egg
1 teaspoon cinnamon
1 teaspoon mixed spice
2 ozs caster sugar (50 g)
½ pint of milk (275 ml)
1 teaspoon sugar

To glaze:
> A little beaten egg

In a large bowl, mix together all the dry ingredients and leave in a warm place such as the airing cupboard.

Warm the milk to body temperature and put half of it in a jug with the teaspoon of sugar. Crumble in the yeast and stand it in a warm place to allow it to froth. There are a number of dried yeasts on the market, and these are perfectly acceptable, but you must follow in detail the instructions on the packets and have a lot of patience, in my experience.

Just before you are ready to start the mixing process, when the yeast has frothed, beat the egg well and add it to the rest of the warmed milk.

Make a well in the centre of the dried ingredients and confidently pour in the liquids. Fold the dried ingredients into the centre to make a dough. Knead it well.

Divide the mixture into smaller pieces, about half the size you want your buns to be, and place them on a greased baking tray. Put them back in the airing cupboard or wherever until they double in size.

Brush the buns with a little beaten egg and cut the tops with a knife, making the sign of the cross.

Bake in the oven (preheated to 450 f, Gas 8, 230 c) for fifteen to twenty minutes.

Serve while still warm, spread thickly with butter.

# Family · Feasting

# BREAD

'Strengthen your heart with a morsel of
bread . . .'

*Judges Chapter Nineteen*

There are numerous references to bread in the
Bible, and today, more than ever before,
there are a wide selection of breads available.
Here are a number of recipes which I hope
are interesting to try. You don't need to be
an expert baker to have a go at them.

## RECIPES:

*Wholewheat bread*
*Malt bread*
*Herb bread*
*Soda bread*

My earliest adventures at breadmaking (for *adventures* they truly have been), have almost left me scarred. Not in any physical way, but with fear!

In one of our houses in Suffolk, we had an old 'Dutch' oven with a brick lining which had been used to cook bread for centuries. The art was to get the old roof of the oven white hot and then pop in the bread (which had proved) to bake for a final thirty or forty minutes.

Alas, we never managed to use this oven, although I am sure it would have made superb bread, but we did have friends who made their bread in a similar oven. Later, they wanted to alter the house, but found that the oven had baked the clay it was made of so hard that they had to use a small charge of dynamite to remove it! It's a wonder they didn't reduce the rest of the house to rubble as well.

My best breadmaking experiences were on a Sunday morning, after church, in a Surrey vicarage where the vicar's wife managed to cope with preparing Sunday lunch for a large family and making bread rolls all at the same time. Once she had taught me the lesson: *Be patient and don't worry about it*, I was well away. On the market now, of course, there are many fine bread flours available and this has made the whole bread making experience a greater pleasure. And the aroma of bread baking has always made home feel a more secure place for me somehow.

So I would suggest that if you have never made bread before, you start now, right this minute! If the shops are shut then go out first thing in the morning and buy the stuff you need. In the meantime, go and have a look at what you have got in the kitchen . . . you may be half way there already.

# Wholewheat bread

3 lbs wholewheat flour (1 kg 350 g)
1 teaspoon salt
a little less than 1½ pints of warm water
  (845 ml)
2 ozs dried yeast (50 g)
1 teaspoon honey

Mix together the salt and the flour in a warmed
basin. Leave them in the airing cupboard or
somewhere similar for a few minutes.

In a quarter of a pint of water, dissolve the
honey and the yeast and leave in a warm place
to froth up. Warm the rest of the water up to the
temperature of the yeast mixture. Make a well in
the mound of warmed flour and add the yeast
mixture and the warmed water. Begin to mix the
flour and the liquids together immediately. Some
flours will need more or less water, but I always
reckon it is best to underestimate at first rather
than go over the top and put in too much all at
once.

Eventually you will have a firm ball of dough
which you should be able to knead easily. The
dough should not be too sticky – if it is, add some
more flour, and if it is a bit lumpy, very carefully
add some more water, but make sure it is warm
water. Knead for a few minutes.

Put the dough back in the bowl, cover it with
a damp cloth and leave in a warm place to double
in size . . . that is optimistic I always find, so I

only expect it to grow by half as much again. It should take about an hour.

Remove the dough from the bowl and knead well again on a floured board or table. This is called 'knocking the dough back'. Divide the dough then between three one-pound (450 g) loaf tins and allow to prove (that is to rise again . . . you can see the Biblical connection!) The tins should be about two-thirds full of dough before they have risen again. Pop them in a hot oven 400 f, Gas 6, 200 c, and after ten minutes turn the oven down to 350 f, Gas 4, 180 c, and allow to cook for another thirty or forty minutes. If the loaves are cooked, the tins will sound hollow when tapped, and the smell will be irresistible. Allow to cool on a rack. These loaves will freeze superbly.

The dough can also be made into rolls. Bake these on a baking tray.

# Malt bread

1½ lb wholewheat flour (700 g)
4 ozs chopped walnuts (110 g)
8 ozs raisins (225 g)
½ oz dried yeast (10 g)
3 tablespoons malt extract
2 teaspoons molasses
1½ pints of warm water (or 300 ml)

Put all the dry ingredients except the yeast into a large bowl and leave in a warm place. To a quarter of a pint (150 ml) of warm water, add the yeast and to the other quarter pint (150 ml) add the molasses and malt extract. When the yeast has frothed up, mix both liquids into the flour mixture and knead the dough well. Cover with a damp cloth and leave to rise until it is half its size again. Then 'knock it back'. Divide the dough between two 1½ lb (700 g) loaf tins and let it prove. Bake at 450 f, Gas 8, 230 c, for about twenty-five minutes.

Delicious warm or cold spread with butter.

# Herb bread

1¼ lb wholewheat flour (560 g)
4 ozs medium oatmeal (110 g)
2 ozs sunflower seeds (50 g)
½ oz dried yeast (10 g)
1½ teaspoons dried rosemary
2 teaspoons honey
1 dessertspoon melted butter
1 pint of warm water (570 ml)

Mix together all the dry ingredients except the
yeast. Leave to warm through in an airing
cupboard or other warm place. Heat the water to
blood temperature and add the honey and yeast,
together with the melted butter. Make a well in
the flour and pour in the mixture when it has
gone frothy. Make your dough, and knead it.

Leave to rise and then 'knock back'.

Divide the dough into two, and make what
shapes you will. I usually make two plaits: this
requires six strings of dough, three for each plait.

Allow to prove, or rise again, and bake at 400 f,
Gas 6, 200 c, for about thirty-five minutes.

This bread is a perfect accompaniment to cheese
or hot soups.

# Soda bread

2 lb wholewheat flour (900 g)
½ oz salt (10 g)
2 teaspoons baking powder
1 teaspoon cream of tartar
1 teaspoon bicarbonate of soda
2 ozs melted butter (50 g)
1 pint of sour milk, warmed (570 ml)

Mix all the dry ingredients together and leave to stand in a warm place. When warmed through, make a well in the middle and add the milk and melted butter. Mix as quickly and lightly as you can, so as not to squeeze out all the air.

Divide into two rounds and place on an oiled baking sheet. Brush with milk and bake at 400 f, Gas 6, 200 c, for forty-five minutes.

Perfect with butter and strawberry jam.

# WINES & CORDIALS

'Royal wine in abundance . . .'
*Esther Chapter One*

Not what you may at first think: a selection of the grand cuvées of France, but a few gentle hints on how to have fun with the home-made products (alcoholic and non-alcoholic) . . . pea pod wine for instance!

## RECIPES:

*Barley wine*
*Pea pod wine*
*Jungle juice*
*Apple wine*
*Lemon squash*
*Elderflower cordial*
*Advocaat*
*The Bishop*
*Gabriel's nectar*
*St. Patrick's pleasure*
*An Irish cream*

I could not resist adding this little section of home-made wines and cordials as they are so simple. But you do need patience to achieve the best results. Be guided much more by the timetable of wine-making than anything else. The results can be fascinating and very enjoyable.

No doubt near your home, there will be a wine-making club, and you can obtain lots of tips as well as happy encouragement from fellow home-brewers. Or if you have a curate, ask him . . . they nearly always know about these things! Not like us vicars . . . we are far too busy . . . cooking!

The recipes for wine that you will find here are indeed simple and can be made without a great deal of fuss and usually with excellent results.

The other drinks are for the younger (or teetotal) members of the family except, of course, those with a generous measure of alcohol in them. The Irish Cream is given to me quite regularly by one of my parishioners to whom I take communion at home. She is a delightful lady and it is always waiting there for me as I walk in, hidden in the kitchen. 'Would you like a little drop of, er . . . Vicar?' she says. We have never got round to mentioning its name, but the recipe was freely given, as are liberal doses of this mixture if I don't stop her!

# Barley wine

1 lb barley (450 g)
1 lb raisins (450 g)
1 lb old potatoes (450 g)
4 lb white sugar (1.8 kg)
1 oz yeast (25 g)
1 gallon of hot water (not boiling) (4.5 litres)

Into a clean plastic bucket, cut up the potatoes
and add the raisins, barley and sugar. Stir well
and cover.

Dissolve the yeast in the water and pour into
the bucket. Leave covered over for six weeks
with muslin and stir every day.

Strain the wine and bottle it and keep it for six
months before drinking.

Make it in the spring and you will have a barley
wine for harvest time!

# Pea pod wine

Quite often known as the poor man's Chablis!

2 gallons of pea pods (minus the peas) (9.1 litres)
4 lb sugar (1.8 kg)
1 gallon of water (4.5 litres)
½ oz yeast (10 g)

Boil the pods in the water until they are yellow, and strain them. Dissolve the sugar in the cooking liquid and allow it to cool for a short time so that the yeast will not be killed when it is added. First mix the yeast with a little of the liquid before adding it to the whole.

Pour the liquid into a demijohn and leave to ferment for about twenty-one days. Filter and bottle. The wine will be cloudy at first (so much like the English weather), but it will slowly clear and be ready for drinking after about six months.

It is best served very chilled.

# Jungle juice

6 large navel oranges
½ lb raisins (225 g)
1 lb wheat (450 g)
4 lbs old potatoes (1.8 kg)
4 lb sugar (1.8 kg)
1 oz yeast (25 g)
10 pints of water. (5.75 litres)

Take three pints (1.75 litres) of water and cut up the oranges into it and boil for about ten minutes. Stand this liquid to one side.

Slice the potatoes thinly and bring them to the boil in seven pints (4 litres) of water. Simmer gently for 10 minutes. Remove the scum as it rises to the surface with a serrated spoon or sieve. Strain off the water into a large container and add the sugar and the yeast after it has cooled a little.

Strain the orange water and add it to the potato water. Pour into demijohns and ferment out with the aid of an air lock.

Once again, do not be in too much of a hurry, and leave it fermenting about a year before you filter and bottle it.

# Apple wine

six pounds of sweet apples (2.75 kg)
10 pints of water (5.75 litres)
1 lb rice (450 g)
1 lb dates, roughly chopped (450 g)
2 oranges
4 lb brown sugar (1.8 kg)

Wash the apples in cold water and bring them to
the boil in the water. Boil for about fifteen or
twenty minutes and then remove from the water.
Add the rice and boil for three minutes and then
strain and add the dates. Cut up the oranges and
add these to the mixture with all their juices.
Add the sugar whilst the liquid is still hot and let
it dissolve.

Pour this mixture into demijohns and let it
ferment with an air lock in place. This will take
various lengths of time depending on the time of
the year but whatever you do, do not be in a
hurry to drink it, the longer you leave it the
better.

When one summer has passed and the autumn
winds blow, filter the juice and bottle it. It really
is deliciously simple.

Various kinds of apple produce different
results. I was very pleased with the Russets I
bought for the purpose. We enjoyed very tasty
and very unusual wine from them.

# Lemon squash

the juice and rind of 4 lemons
2 ozs citric acid (50 g)
3 lbs sugar (1.35 kg)
4 pints of water (2.3 litres)

Pour the water into a large saucepan and add the grated lemon rind. Bring to the boil, and bubble for one minute. Meanwhile, empty the sugar and the citric acid into a large bowl. Squeeze the juice of the lemons over this and then pour on the hot lemony water. Stir to dissolve the sugar, and cool before straining and bottling and using as any other squash.

It is possible to use this recipe with grapefruit as well.

# Elderflower cordial

25 heads of elderflowers
2 ozs tartaric acid (50 g)
4 oranges, sliced
1 lemon, sliced
3 pints of water (1.75 litres)
1½ lbs sugar (700 g)

Boil the water, add the sugar and stir until it is
dissolved. Add the sliced oranges and lemon and
the tartaric acid. Leave the mixture to cool, and
then add the elderflower heads.

Leave to stand for two days, stirring regularly.
After this, strain the mixture and squeeze the
juice out of the flower heads. Bottle, and use as
a cordial as required.

This tastes best when diluted with tonic water.

# Advocaat

6 eggs
½ pint of sherry (275 ml)
1 miniature of brandy
1 large tin of condensed milk

Whip the eggs well and add the condensed milk whipping again thoroughly. A liquidiser or food processor is ideal for this. Slowly pour in the sherry and the brandy and blend all together. Strain into a bottle and serve well chilled. This is especially good if you are feeling under the weather.

# The Bishop

A traditional old recipe that must go back to the time when port was first introduced into this country. Please do not use the best vintage port for this cup; one of the cheaper supermarket varieties will do extremely well.

Serve this as a treat for the carol singers or other visitors on a winter's evening . . . but be careful, they'll soon come back for more!

2 lemons
12 cloves
2 pints of port (1.25 litres)
1 pint of water (570 ml)
1 level teaspoon ground mixed spice
2 ozs lump sugar (50 g)

Stick one of the lemons with the cloves, just as if you were going to make a pomander. Place this spiced lemon in an oven at 350 f, Gas 4, 180 c, and leave for about thirty minutes.

In a saucepan, boil the water with the spices for a minute.

In another saucepan, heat the port until it almost reaches boiling point and add the spiced lemon and the spiced water along with the lumps of sugar. Carefully pare some of the rind off the other lemon and add its juice to the mixture.

This cup should be served as hot as possible and where appropriate, with shortbread.

# Gabriel's nectar

6 eggs
½ pint of medium sherry (275 ml)
½ pint of single cream (275 ml)
1 miniature of brandy

Whip the eggs well, add the cream and whip
again. Add the sherry and the brandy and beat
well with a hand whisk.

If you wish to give the final result a more
professional touch (which really is not necessary
– it just adds to the aesthetic value), add a little
yellow food colouring.

It is important to keep this in the refrigerator
once it is made and advisable that this is
consumed within a fortnight. Don't worry, as
that is quite possible!

# St. Patrick's pleasure

I have a confession to make . . . I have never been to Ireland. However, I have been told that this is a truly Irish recipe . . . at least, it is warming and welcoming like the Irish. I first came across it on my communion round when we take the sacrament to the ill or housebound. One of my parishioners convinced me I ought to try this, and I have been a convert ever since.

3 eggs
1 dessertspoon instant coffee
1 large tin of condensed milk
½ pint of single cream (275 ml)
1 cup of whisky

Place all the ingredients in a mixing bowl and blend them together very gently with a hand whisk. Some people like to whip the eggs up a little first. Do not use an electric mixer or it may become too thick.

Strain the liquid twice through a nylon sieve and then bottle. As there are fresh ingredients in this it is advisable to store the liqueur in a refrigerator. But beware, it will not keep long in any case . . . the angels will have their share!

# An Irish cream

10 fl ozs of fresh single cream (275 ml)
3 ozs caster sugar (75 g)
5 fl ozs of condensed milk (150 ml)
3 eggs
1 dessertspoon 'Camp' coffee or instant coffee
   mixed with a little hot water
1 large cup of whisky

In a food processor or blender, blend the eggs
and sugar together.
   Add the cream and the coffee and mix well.
   Add the whisky and mix again.
   Bottle and store in the refrigerator.

# Bible cake ingredients:

½ lb butter (225 g)
½ lb sugar (225 g)
1 tablespoon honey
3 eggs
½ lb raisins (225 g)
½ lb figs, chopped (225 g)
2 ozs almonds, chopped (50 g)
1 lb flour (450 g)
spice
salt
1 teaspoon baking powder
1 tablespoon milk or water

# Index